MW00777648

Wholeheartedly

A Chronological Journey through the Bible in One Year

Allison T. Cain

Wholeheartedly
A Chronological Journey through the Bible in One Year

Published 2016. All rights reserved.

Scripture quotations are from Reading God's Story, A Chronological Daily Bible (HCSB), copyright © 1999, 2000, 2002, 2003, 2009 by Holman Bible Publishers.

Scripture taken from the English Standard Version Study Bible, Copyright 2008 © by Good News Publishers.

Scripture quotations are from the Holy Bible, New International Version, copyright © 1973, 1978, 1984 by International Bible Society.

Scripture taken from THE MESSAGE. Copyright © 1993, 1994, 1995, 1996, 2000, 2001, 2002. Used by permission of NavPress Publishing Group.

Allison Cain [www.allisonTcain.com]
Copyright © 2016 by Allison T. Cain

ISBN- 978-0692746219
FIRST PRINTING

To order additional copies of this resource, visit www.allisonTcain.com
for store locations, www.amazon.com.

Editor – Mallory Russell
Photographer – Sara Grow, Growphotography.com
Cover Art – Kent Swecker
Printed in the United States of America

For my dear friend, mentor, coach and now adopted family mentor whose generous Christmas gift of the HCSB Chronological Bible inspired my journey from Genesis to Revelation.

Grover, without you this book wouldn't be possible. Thank you for challenging me, encouraging me and providing thought-provoking conversations that I will forever treasure.

Wholeheartedly
A Chronological Journey through the Bible in One Year

Introduction

These devotions share my thoughts, feelings and discoveries of the things I forgot, overlooked or never considered. Some were obvious but needed revisiting and others were so strange and curious they needed further investigation.

Throughout my 30s and 40s God has revealed some pretty amazing, yet simple, ways to make scripture come alive. I share these tools in my book *In the Mi[God]dle: Keys to Keeping God in the Middle of All We Think Do and Say*, and also when I have opportunities to speak to women's groups. However, God has opened my eyes to another incredible and easy way to study scripture that has brought me so much closer to Him: reading the Bible chronologically.

Not only has studying the Bible chronologically given me a deeper understanding of the thread God has woven through history, but it has also provided me with an intense appreciation for Him in my daily life and world events.

By God's grace, I never doubt His existence, power or attention to detail. However, I do sometimes place Him in my human box when He is so much more; so much greater. By simplifying His magnitude, I forget to look at Him with the awe, gratitude, praise and adoration that I should.

Not only did I read the Bible in chronological order, but I read it in a translation I'd never read (Holman – HCSB). Approaching the Bible through these two new lenses was incredible.

I can hardly put into words how much it has impacted my walk with Christ and my understanding of the scriptures. Simply put, reading the Bible chronologically has made me want to dance like David in pure abandon, without a care of who is watching and throwing every bit of energy, love and might I have into worshiping our Creator.

Here are just a few things that the LORD has opened my eyes to since I began this journey:

- It's a story. I know we already know that, but there is something about reading the story in order that makes it so much better! Imagine reading one of your favorite books out of order. Things don't make as much sense and are inevitably more difficult to grasp (i.e. historical timelines, descendants, story lines). There have been times I've been so excited about "the story" that I've completed a week's worth of reading in one sitting because I couldn't put it down.

- Similar to the Gospels, did you know that Chronicles and Kings repeat many of the same stories? Perhaps you know more than I did, but I never realized this. When reading these books back to back, it reinforces the story and offers additional perspectives with small changes in words and details.

- Imagine reading in 1 Chronicles, which is all about David's life and inevitable struggles and sins, in context with the Psalms he wrote during each season. They immediately take on an entirely new meaning, full of depth and beauty when placed in context. Consider this: it's easy to enjoy a song through listening, but if you read the artist's personal journal and discover why the song was written, it comes alive in a new way.

- When you read the Bible in the order it was written, you receive a fresh glimpse into how God's hand really is in every detail. It's not just a saying anymore. It's real. You see His hand at work as each leader or king gains or loses his power. You see how God raises up the shepherd's son and understand how it all ties together.

This is just a taste of all God showed me through my chronological journey. I pray you will consider purchasing a chronological (HCSB) Bible as you begin this study. Or (if you are more patient than I am) you can follow along the chronological reading plan I include in each week. If you choose the latter, be prepared to do a lot of turning and flipping of pages. Please let me know if you decide to take this journey, as I would love to pray for you along the way. You can contact me through my website at www.allisonTcain.com.

How to use this book

I'm not a researcher in the research and report sense. I prefer to discover and report. I like to document the thoughts and emotions that ebb and flow inside me as scriptures wash over my soul. What is God teaching me at this moment in His text? What does He desire for me to know? To trust in? To understand? These are the thoughts, questions and experiences that pull me back to scripture over and over again.

This isn't your typical devotional or Bible study. It's set up to guide you through the Bible each week in chronological order. Along with that reading plan is space for your own notes as well as some of my insights for you to read along that way. Questions that I pondered and realizations that came to me to inspire and encourage you to stay the course even when the words don't seem to make sense or the text becomes repetitive. These discoveries are real and pure moments of my own that I hope will inspire and guide you during your own time. For that reason, you will notice that there are a few weeks that have one devotion with your reading and other weeks that have more.

The notes section will be divided into five sections:

Revelations: If you have read these passages before, what did notice for the first time? Or if this is your first time in these passages, what jumped out at you?

Questions: What questions come to mind about the setting, meaning or characters you are reading about? Don't worry about the answers right now, simply make note of your questions.

Repeats: What word or theme is being repeated?

Deeper Study: What do I want to study more about later? Is it research to answer one of your questions or dig deeper into a revelation or repeated theme and how God is using it to speak into your life?

Etc.: Other thoughts I need to put into writing.

I encourage you to jump into this adventure WHOLEHEARTEDLY! In other words, with an unconditional commitment, unstinting devotion and wild enthusiasm. Don't get frustrated or give up if you fall behind. You will start out strong, Leviticus will nearly make you quit all together, but keep plugging away. I promise you will never be more excited about the Bible story, especially when you turn that page to find Jesus in the New Testament. You will discover and unravel mysteries you never noticed. You will find treasures on every page and learn more than you ever imagined about your Heavenly Father.

Don't be afraid to get ahead if time permits. If it takes you two years instead of one, who cares?! Make this yours, but seek God though His word. Pray He multiplies your time and understanding in ways you never imagined to complete this journey. For as It says in John 15:

Remain in me, as I also remain in you. No branch can bear fruit by itself; it must remain in the vine. Neither can you bear fruit unless you remain in me. John 15:4

Remain (v.): to be left when the other parts are gone or have been used; to be something that still needs to be done, dealt with, etc.; to stay in the same place or with the same person or group: to stay after others have gone.

The word of God never grows old or stale. It is always fresh and relevant. I pray you will remain in Him wholeheartedly during the course of this study and revel in His truths and promises He will reveal to your obedient heart.

Week 1

- ☐ Monday - Genesis 1-3
- ☐ Tuesday - Genesis 4-7
- ☐ Wednesday - Genesis 8-11
- ☐ Thursday - Job 1-5
- ☐ Friday - Job 6-9
- ☐ Saturday - Job 10-13
- ☐ Sunday- Job 14-16

Week 2

- ☐ Monday - Job 17-20
- ☐ Tuesday - Job 21-23
- ☐ Wednesday - Job 24-28
- ☐ Thursday - Job 29-31
- ☐ Friday - Job 32-34
- ☐ Saturday - Job 35-37
- ☐ Sunday - Job 38-39

Revelations	
Questions	
Repeats	
Deeper Study	
Etc.	

A Divine Appointment

So the heavens and the earth and everything in them were completed. By the seventh day God completed His work that He had done, and He rested on the seventh day from all His work that He had done. [3] God blessed the seventh day and declared it holy, for on it He rested from His work of creation. Genesis 2:1-3

We serve an amazing God, who stretched out the heavens, laid the foundation of the earth, and formed the human spirit within a person (Zechariah 12:1). It saddens me to see the mystery and awe of our Creator missing in the hearts of His people. Sometimes it feels as if we are so burdened down with past sins, guilt, shame or legalism that we lose sight of how incredible our God has been and always will be. Not only did He create all of Heaven and Earth, but He left us a collection of books we call the Bible that tells the story of His broken people and His great love for us. From Genesis to Revelation, the theme stays true. God's love for us has defeated death and although we may feel as though we are losing the battle, God has already won the war. Amen!

So, as you begin this adventure through the story of God please consider that the creator of the Universe, the one who knew you before you were born, the one who knows every hair on your head, loves you and wants to sit down with you. How quickly would you drop everything on your calendar and pull out your credit card to buy a plane ticket if your favorite band, movie star, president or author called to have you over to their home for dinner and conversation?

Well, your Heavenly Father created this whole Universe. He's the top dog, the CEO of life, the alpha and the omega. He is the one who holds your life breath in His hand. He loves you so much that He sent His very own son, His only son, to die so that you could live forever with Him in paradise. And … He wants to know you better. He wants to sit down with you and hear your heart's desires. He wants to show you His promises of comfort, peace, love, forgiveness and grace. He desires for you to seek Him when you need wisdom and direction. He wants to be your living well. Your stream in the desert. Your lifeline and your listening ear. He will not judge you, but He will love you. He will not disgrace you, but He will give you comfort. He will not condemn you, but He will forgive you.

In Hebrew, "word" in the verb tense means "speak." So consider this, when you are in the word of God it is God speaking to you. Allow God to guide and direct your heart through your time in the Bible this year. I sometimes pray that God will slap me in the face with an answer because I don't want to miss Him speaking to me, and challenge you to pray the same while believing He will answer. I trust if anyone can get through this stubborn head of mine, it is the Creator of the Universe. Are you ready for your divine appointment?

Are You Hiding?

Now the serpent was the most cunning of all the wild animals that the LORD God had made. He said to the woman, "Did God really say, 'You can't eat from any tree in the garden'?" Genesis 3:1

It all started here! Adam and Eve, the forbidden fruit, sneaky serpent and the fall of man. The topic of Adam and Eve comes up often because sin is such an ongoing issue for each of us. Since the day they made the decision to eat the fruit, life hasn't been all fun and games for the rest of humanity. It's easy to think if we had been the first ones in the garden, we would have never touched that forbidden fruit, but I'm not convinced. Even in the safety of church or small group I fight sinful thoughts and desires. But that's not what struck me this time as I read these familiar verses from Genesis.

Then the man and his wife heard the sound of the LORD God walking in the garden at the time of the evening breeze, and they hid themselves from the LORD God among the trees of the garden. So the LORD God called out to the man and said to him, "Where are you?" And he said, "I heard You in the garden and I was afraid because I was naked, so I hid." Genesis 3:8-10

To hide means *to put, keep out of sight or conceal from the view or notice of others*. Adam and Eve hid themselves from God after their eyes were open to sin. This reminded me of how often we try to hide or conceal feelings, sin, worldly desires or failures not just from those we love or work with, but from God too. The irony is that we cannot hide anything from God. He might go along with us and ask, "Where are you?" like a parent playing hide and seek with a two year old you can visibly see hiding behind the small skinny tree, but He knows everything.

This is just one of the things to adore about our Heavenly Father! He knows all our weaknesses, sinful desires, failures and shameful thoughts, yet loves us anyway. He sent His only Son to die for us knowing all of these things already. We should ask ourselves, "When do I hide? What do I try to hide?"

Once we recognize these things, we can name them and the power they have over us grows weaker and weaker. It's time we take off the masks and stop hiding from the only One who loves us despite all we do, think, say and feel. It's time to allow ourselves the freedom to share some faults and failures with others so that we can grow in humility and others will know they are not alone. So, let's pray for one another. No more hiding. Put what's been in the dark out into God's healing light, and let Him begin to work in your heart like never before.

 Notes and Reflections:

Week 3

- ☐ Monday - Job 40-42
- ☐ Tuesday - Genesis 12-15
- ☐ Wednesday - Genesis 16-18
- ☐ Thursday - Genesis 19-21
- ☐ Friday - Genesis 22-24
- ☐ Saturday - Genesis 25-26
- ☐ Sunday - Genesis 27-29

Week 4

- ☐ Monday - Genesis 30-31
- ☐ Tuesday - Genesis 32-34
- ☐ Wednesday - Genesis 35-37
- ☐ Thursday - Genesis 38-40
- ☐ Friday - Genesis 41-42
- ☐ Saturday - Genesis 43-45
- ☐ Sunday - Genesis 46-47

Revelations	
Questions	
Repeats	
Deeper Study	
Etc.	

Covenants & Stones

One thing is for sure, you can discover some odd things when you read the Old Testament (OT). Today I want to talk about one odd thing and one beautiful thing that stood out to me as I was reading through Genesis. It's amazing how you can read through a book of the Bible and miss something over and over again until God gives you eyes to see.

He said to the senior servant in his household, the one in charge of all that he had, "Put your hand under my thigh. I want you to swear by the LORD, the God of heaven and the God of earth, that you will not get a wife for my son from the daughters of the Canaanites, among whom I am living, but will go to my country and my own relatives and get a wife for my son Isaac." Genesis 24:2-4

Wait? What? Did you see it? Here it is again:

When the time drew near for Israel to die, he called for his son Joseph and said to him, "If I have found favor in your eyes, put your hand under my thigh and promise that you will show me kindness and faithfulness. Do not bury me in Egypt." Genesis 47:29

"Put your hand under my thigh and promise." I have to admit this didn't initially catch my attention in Genesis 24, but when it was repeated in Genesis 47, I went back to take a look and did a little research. It seemed strange to me. We raise our right hand when swearing these days, but apparently, swearing on one's testicles (thigh/loins) was common in OT times. There are a few different schools of thought on why they did this, but the most common explanation was that that thighs (or loins) were considered a source of prosperity. Think about how important it was for God's people to multiply and increase their numbers (with children) in early Biblical times. Although we are taught in the New Testament "do not swear—not by heaven or by earth or by anything else. All you need to say is a simple 'Yes' or 'No' Otherwise you will be condemned," swearing an oath was common and accepted and practiced in the OT (James 5:12).

Stone Markers were another interesting concept that repeated itself and stood out to me during my reading in Genesis.

Although I had noted this ritual before, it seemed to have a deeper impact on me as I read it this time. From Genesis 28–35 we see how Jacob used stone markers to record important events, milestones and covenants.

In Genesis 28:10-22 after God comes to Jacob in a dream he says, **"When Jacob awoke from his sleep, he said, "Surely the LORD is in this place, and I did not know it." (v.16)** and then **"Early in the morning Jacob took the stone that was near his head and set it up as a marker. He poured oil on top of it and named the place Bethel, though previously the city was named Luz" (v.18-19).**

In Genesis 31:13 God even says to Jacob, **"I am the God of Bethel, where you poured oil on the stone marker and made a solemn vow to Me. Get up, leave this land, and return to your native land."**

When Jacob and Laban made a covenant to end a dispute in Genesis 31:44-46, Jacob said, "'**Come now, let's make a covenant, you and I. Let it be a witness between the two of us.' So Jacob picked out a stone and set it up as a marker. Then Jacob said to his relatives, 'Gather stones.' And they took stones and made a mound, then ate there by the mound."**

We see this again in Genesis 35:14 when God spoke to Jacob, **"[Jacob] set up a marker at the place where He had spoken to him—a stone marker. He poured a drink offering on it and anointed it with oil."**

I hope sharing these verses emphasizes Jacob's use of stones to signify or proclaim a memory. As I think back on my life, I can think of many times where I would have placed a stone marker because I felt His presence was close. He helped me overcome an obstacle that had hindered living my life for His glory or even the mending of a relationship that seemed like it could never be restored.

As we close today, I hope you will sit and reflect back on the moments in your life that you feel are worthy of a stone marker. Maybe even write them down on a paper to keep inside your Bible and continue to add to them as the years go by because, as Jacob said so beautifully, **"Surely the LORD is in this place, and I did not know it." Genesis 28:16**

    Notes and Reflections:

Week 5

- ☐ Monday - Genesis 48-50
- ☐ Tuesday - Exodus 1-3
- ☐ Wednesday - Exodus 4-6
- ☐ Thursday - Exodus 7-9
- ☐ Friday - Exodus 10-12
- ☐ Saturday - Exodus 13-15
- ☐ Sunday - Exodus 16-18

Week 6

- ☐ Monday - Exodus 19-21
- ☐ Tuesday - Exodus 22-24
- ☐ Wednesday - Exodus 25-27
- ☐ Thursday - Exodus 28-29
- ☐ Friday - Exodus 30-32
- ☐ Saturday - Exodus 33-35
- ☐ Sunday - Exodus 36-38

Revelations	
Questions	
Repeats	
Deeper Study	
Etc.	

Who Me?

Yes, you! It never ceases to inspire me as I read the Bible and discover all the average, fragile and "normal" people God calls to accomplish His most amazing feats. First, there was Moses who said to the Lord when He called on him, **"Who am I that I should go to Pharaoh and bring the Israelites out of Egypt?" (Exodus 3:11).**

God wanted Moses to talk Pharaoh into letting His people go. He wanted them released from slavery and called on Moses to make it happen. Moses said to the Lord, **"Pardon your servant, LORD. I have never been eloquent, neither in the past nor since you have spoken to your servant. I am slow of speech and tongue" (Exodus 4:10).**

Oh, how I can relate to Moses. There have been more times than I would like to admit that I've said to the Lord, "Are you sure you have the right person?" I struggled with writing in school, public speaking used to be one of my biggest fears and let's not even talk about my past! Whew! This unworthy servant joins the ranks of so many others that came before. Then there was Gideon, who after the Lord handed over the Israelites to Midian for seven years, called upon him to deliver the Israelites from Midian.

"Pardon me, my LORD," Gideon replied, "but how can I save Israel? My clan is the weakest in Manasseh, and I am the least in my family" (Judges 6:15).

God continued His pattern, and chose Gideon who was weak and young and it doesn't stop with Gideon. Throughout the Bible from Genesis to Revelation God does this. We haven't even gotten to David who defeats Goliath (1 Samuel 14). God literally uses the weak to lead the strong. It's how He rolls, as my kids would say. Through our weakness and submission to Him, He can do a great work in us and through us for His glory. I dare say, in ways we would have never imagined or asked for.

But he said to me, "My grace is sufficient for you, for my power is made perfect in weakness." Therefore I will boast all the more gladly about my weaknesses, so that Christ's power may rest on me. That is why, for Christ's sake, I delight in weaknesses, in insults, in hardships, in persecutions, in difficulties. For when I am weak, then I am strong (2 Corinthians 12:9-10).

Be assured that if God calls you, He will equip you. Don't believe your past is too broken, your courage too fragile or that you don't have what it takes to serve our Lord. He is calling all of us in one way or another to share our faith, to be the light in this dark world and to love our neighbors as ourselves. Will you trust? Will you follow His lead?

Why Harden Their Hearts?

As we continue on my path to remain in God, His word, His plans and the gifts He has given, God is giving me sweet confirmations of my return to a more discovery-based (instead of research) study plan.

A dear friend of mine, from years ago, recently came back into my life. It was such a blessing to reconnect with her after losing touch when I left the workforce 10 years ago. About a month after we reconnected she had a scare and ended up in the ER where she discovered she has a brain tumor. It is operable, but was a very long and tricky surgery. I have no doubt God orchestrated our reconnection at this exact time so that I could be in her life during this time. As we sat in her living room a few weeks ago discussing all she has to do and prepare for before surgery she said, "I have to do end of life preparation, too. I was thinking you could lead my service if need be." She explained that not only did I know her, but I know the Bible with my heart not just my mind.

I realized that what I was beginning to see as a weakness in myself and my biblical study wasn't at all. It's a gift to feel the scriptures. Yes, we need to understand and be careful not to misrepresent the Bible. We need to uncover the context, but are not required to attend divinity school to study, understand, and breathe in God's word. Rather than fearing what we don't know or understand, we need to ask questions and pray for God to open our eyes.

Please hear me when I confidently say you can open the Bible and study God's word on your own. He hopes you will seek Him there, and will undoubtedly reveal Himself to you in unmistakable ways.

One of the most recent questions that burdened my heart during my yearly reading plan was when God called Moses to deliver His people out of Egypt and Pharaoh's control, why did God keep hardening Pharaoh's heart so that he wouldn't comply with Moses? God could have made this easy on His people by just letting them go or easier on Moses by having Pharaoh comply much sooner. This "hardening of heart" theme followed throughout the story.

The LORD said to Moses, "When you return to Egypt, see that you perform before Pharaoh all the wonders I have given you the power to do. But I will harden his heart so that he will not let the people go. Then say to Pharaoh, 'This is what the LORD says: Israel is my firstborn son, and I told you, 'Let my son go, so he may worship me.' But you refused to let him go; so I will kill your firstborn son" (Exodus 4:21-23).

It doesn't stop there. Even later in **Exodus 14:3-4** after Pharaoh finally succumbs to all the plagues and deaths of firstborn sons and lets Moses take his people, God tells Moses,

Pharaoh will think, 'The Israelites are wandering around the land in confusion, hemmed in by the desert.' And I will harden Pharaoh's heart, and he will pursue them.

And even still, once the Israelites are finally released, God continues to harden Pharaoh's heart. Why did God keep doing this? He could have made it so easy for Moses to free the Israelites and instead He says over and over "I'll harden his heart so he won't grant your request." Do you think Moses was thinking, as we sometimes do, "Thanks a lot, God. You are all powerful so why can't this be a little easier?" The answer is there if we keep reading to verse 4 and it's glorious.

But I will gain glory for myself through Pharaoh and all his army, and the Egyptians will know that I am the LORD." So the Israelites did this.

Again we see in **Exodus 14:31** after the parting of the Red Sea and final escape from Pharaoh:

And when the Israelites saw the mighty hand of the LORD displayed against the Egyptians, the people feared the LORD and put their trust in him and in Moses his servant.

When God makes the impossible happen, you can't mistake His hand is in it. There is no way we can take credit when the miraculous happens and then God receives all the glory. Yes, sometimes it is hard, painstakingly hard. All the pruning, shaping, crushing and molding from what seems like an impossible situation yields fruit when God's hand is in it. When we see God work and know there is no possible way we could have overcome the obstacle or trial on our own our

25

trust grows, our faith is made stronger and our determination to stay the course God has set before us is more obtainable.

If it's all easy, then what do we gain?

To Be Honest

TBH, as my daughter's middle school friends say, it's been a while since I dug down deep into the OT. Since writing the Bible study on Zechariah a few years ago, I've had my head down in the books of the New Testament (NT). Consequently, this journey from beginning to end in the Bible has already been quite a journey. Especially during this time of year (Easter and Lent) my focus is usually on the Gospels and Christ's journey to the cross. Needless to say it's been unusual to be the in books of Leviticus, Exodus, Numbers and Joshua. But, God has opened my eyes and heart to a deeper appreciation for a Savior who took my place on the cross through the reminder of what things looked like for those who lived and worshipped before Christ's amazing sacrifice on the cross.

As I approached this text, I was quickly reminded of how many rules God's first followers had to keep track of and monitor. Honestly, I might have been able to remember and follow it all if I had my iPhone ringing with constant reminders, but those stone tablets and memory were all they had to keep track of the 613 commandments/law (also called the "Torah" or "Law of Moses"). Honestly, we can hardly handle the 10 commandments. Can you imagine 613?

Many of us are familiar with the guidelines from Leviticus 11 on what to eat and not eat, but did you know they had guidelines in great detail on how to deal with scabs, burns, hair loss and even mildew outbreaks (Leviticus 13 & 14). This is just the beginning. As you can imagine, there are many other rules listed for things related to

26

sacrifices, sex, semen, pregnancy, etc. I'll let you dive into some of the others on your own. It boils down to this, God revealed Himself to Moses to present a covenant to His people.

"Then he took the Book of the Covenant and read it to the people. They responded, 'We will do everything the LORD has said; we will obey.' Moses then took the blood, sprinkled it on the people and said, 'This is the blood of the covenant that the LORD has made with you in accordance with all these words.'" Exodus 24:7-8

God offered His people a covenant of protection, provision and prosperity *if* they obeyed His commands as they set out towards the land He promised them. My point this Easter is this: not only did Jesus come and die on a criminal's cross to cover all of our sins, He came to be the ultimate sacrifice and a new beginning for His people. As he sat with the disciples to have the Last Supper, Jesus expressed, **"This cup is the new covenant written in my blood, blood poured out for you" (Luke 22:20).**

Jesus was the final and ultimate sacrifice. The blood He shed was the beginning of a new covenant between God and His people. Don't get me wrong, we still have important guidelines and laws to follow as Christians (10 Commandments, Exodus 20), but God sent His son to wipe away the old covenant that was focused on rules, laws and commands. Christ's death signified a new covenant between God and His children. One not based on the letter of the law, but of the Holy Spirit. A Spirit full of grace, unconditional love and a desire for a personal relationship with each of us.

He has made us competent as ministers of a new covenant—not of the letter but of the Spirit; for the letter kills, but the Spirit gives life. 2 Corinthians 3:6

Jesus replied: "'Love the LORD your God with all your heart and with all your soul and with all your mind.' This is the first and greatest commandment. And the second is like it: 'Love your neighbor as yourself.' All the Law and the Prophets hang on these two commandments." Matthew 22:37-44

I pray you will look at Easter with fresh eyes this year. May they be fixed on the cross and may our hearts always seek our Lord and Savior.

  Notes and Reflections:

Week 7

- [ ] Monday - Exodus 39-40
- [ ] Tuesday - Leviticus 1-4
- [ ] Wednesday - Leviticus 5-7
- [ ] Thursday - Leviticus 8-10
- [ ] Friday - Leviticus 11-13
- [ ] Saturday - Leviticus 14-15
- [ ] Sunday - Leviticus 16-18

Week 8

- [ ] Monday - Leviticus 19-21
- [ ] Tuesday - Leviticus 22-23
- [ ] Wednesday - Leviticus 24-25
- [ ] Thursday - Leviticus 26-27
- [ ] Friday - Numbers 1-2
- [ ] Saturday - Numbers 3-4
- [ ] Sunday - Numbers 5-6

Revelations	
Questions	
Repeats	
Deeper Study	
Etc.	

Burning Anger

I will act with furious hostility toward you; I will also discipline you seven times for your sins. Leviticus 26:28

Then the LORD's anger burned against Moses. Exodus 4:14

Then Balak's anger burned against Balaam. Numbers 24:10

I'm sure you've noticed the theme by now. As I read this week's scriptures I noticed a theme and it continues even into the following weeks. If you look up anger in the Bible, you will find it over and over again. In fact, there are at least 53 (probably more if I keep looking) where it's not just anger, but *burning* anger. Why is anger always burning? I thought about this a lot today. I needed to spend time in God's word exploring anger and how to handle it after a difficult morning with my children. God's word is always right on time. As a mom, it's so frustrating to watch your children do things to one another (on purpose) just to make the other one mad. Thankfully, this isn't the norm and they usually get along, but when they decide to "let the devil win," as we say, it can ruin the entire morning.

I think it's called "burning anger" because, like a fire, it starts slow and as others or life throws kindling on our fire it grows bigger and anger starts rolling like a bonfire started with five dry Christmas trees (trust me on this one – they go up in seconds). Just like this morning, my kids' frustration and purposeful unkindness start to kindle the flames of anger in me. Then as they continued to justify their actions (more kindling), blame one another and yell (gasoline), I had a full blown fire of burning anger.

How do you handle anger? Does it take a lot or just a little to push you over the edge? Honestly, I can handle it for a while when the fire is small, but if things don't resolve and I can't get enough water on the flames, the fire gets out of control and I find myself being burned and falling into the trap letting the anger overtake me. I needed a reminder of what God says about anger. While there are many verses about anger and self-control these stood out to me today.

And the LORD's servant must not be quarrelsome but kind to everyone, able to teach, patiently enduring evil, 2 Timothy 2:24

My dear brothers and sisters, take note of this: Everyone should be quick to listen, slow to speak and slow to become angry, because human anger does not produce the righteousness that God desires. James 1:19-20

Whoever is slow to anger is better than the mighty, and he who rules his spirit than he who takes a city. Proverbs 16:32

An angry person stirs up conflict, and a hot-tempered person commits many sins. Pride brings a person low, but the lowly in spirit gain honor. Proverbs 29:22-23

Be not quick in your spirit to become angry, for anger lodges in the bosom of fools. Ecclesiastes 7:9

Our actions always come down to a heart issue. When we become angry we must look into our hearts and see what is kindling our burning anger. Is it pride, fear, selfishness, a need for control or perhaps all of these things? Thank goodness we have a loving Father who will help us acknowledge and overcome our strongholds. But, we must acknowledge them, pray for forgiveness and ask God to help us weed them out of our hearts. It isn't always pretty in there, but when we face the garbage and are willing to clean it out, everyone benefits. Will you join me?

Father, I pray these scriptures penetrate our hearts and that our thirst for you grows each day, so that living water you provide for us will extinguish all the flames of anger in our lives and that our mouths, actions and thoughts don't overtake us. Father, reveal our strongholds and give us the courage and strength to turn them over to you. Cover us and protect us with your armor so that we can be good examples of your love to everyone around us. Amen

BUT . . .

"Do not seek revenge or bear a grudge against one of your people, but love your neighbor as yourself. I am the LORD." Leviticus 19:18

These words flew off the page at me. Why is this so difficult to forgive sometimes? Why is it easier to love some and more difficult to love others? Why can't everybody just be nice so we don't have to hold grudges? Being a mom of two kids, the three little letters (B-U-T) can drive me absolutely nutty! It's like a whole argument or excuse tied up in one tiny word. "But Mom, he hid my computer." "But Mom, she hit me first … He said I was mean and boring … she told me I couldn't come in her room any more." "But . . but . . but!" It is amazing how my children can use one little word to justify hitting someone, calling someone a name, snatching an item, or breaking another rule we have established in our home. One day, I had enough of the "buts" and pulled out the "but, nothing!" comment. It was inevitable I know, but I try not to pull out those traditional "mom" comments.

As I reflected back on that day, I realized how often I am guilty of the "but" excuse. Not just with others, but with God. Even as adults we try to justify and explain actions and thoughts that we know don't reflect the Kingdom of God. "But, she started a rumor about me … But, he treated me unfairly … But, she lied to me … But, they promised … But, they betrayed my trust … But, I deserve it after all I did for them." Do any of these statements sound familiar?

"But" is just a disclaimer we use that basically means I am accountable unless this happens, except for when or contrary to what you think. There are no buts with God. No excuses. He calls us to forgive. To obey. To trust and to treat others as more important than ourselves. Ugh! This isn't always easy. In fact, a lot of times it seems almost impossible. The only way it is possible is with the power, strength and love of the Holy Spirit.

Today I pray that the Lord will remove the "buts" and excuses from our hearts and fill us with forgiveness, gratitude, love and acceptance for ourselves and those around us.

"But, Nothing!" … I just couldn't resist saying it one more time.

 Notes and Reflections:

Week 9

- ☐ Monday - Numbers 7
- ☐ Tuesday - Numbers 8-10
- ☐ Wednesday - Numbers 11-13
- ☐ Thursday - Numbers 14-15; Psalm 90
- ☐ Friday - Numbers 16-17
- ☐ Saturday - Numbers 18-20
- ☐ Sunday - Numbers 21-22

Week 10

- ☐ Monday - Numbers 23-25
- ☐ Tuesday - Numbers 26-27
- ☐ Wednesday - Numbers 28-30
- ☐ Thursday - Numbers 31-32
- ☐ Friday - Numbers 33-34
- ☐ Saturday - Numbers 35-36
- ☐ Sunday - Deuteronomy 1-2

Revelations	
Questions	
Repeats	
Deeper Study	
Etc.	

After All That?!

Then I said to you, "Do not be terrified; do not be afraid of them. The LORD your God, who is going before you, will fight for you, as he did for you in Egypt, before your very eyes, and in the wilderness. There you saw how the LORD your God carried you, as a father carries his son, all the way you went until you reached this place." In spite of this, you did not trust in the LORD your God, who went ahead of you on your journey, in fire by night and in a cloud by day, to search out places for you to camp and to show you the way you should go. Deuteronomy 1:29-33

As I read the words Moses spoke to the Israelites in Deuteronomy, I was reminded that despite all the amazing miracles of protection and provision they had personally witnessed and received, they still grumbled and doubted. I'm so quick to think, "Surely I wouldn't have turned from the Lord or grumbled at all if I had witnessed all of that personally and not just read about it in the Bible."

Then, I'm reminded or convicted even more quickly of that fact that I'm no different from the Israelites. While it may seem as though the manna that fell, the sea that parted and the cloud by day and fire by night that guided them is so much greater and bolder than what God has done for me, this simply isn't truth.

When I think about the answered prayers for friends, family and healing that have occurred, it blows my mind. What about the time our income and savings were almost out and God provided? Honestly, for us, that was as miraculous as seeing the sea split in two. I've seen relationships restored that I thought never had a chance of reconciliation, addicts become whole and sacrifices made out of love for strangers.

37

All those things and more are just as amazing as what the Israelites witnessed. Yet even after all the ways I've personally experienced God move, there are still days that my heart groans about something that doesn't turn out the way I desired or expected. There are still days I doubt my abilities, talents and example I set. Why do I do this?

I've come to a simple, but honest explanation. We are human! Created in God's image, but only human, not God. That's why Jesus' sacrifice means more and more to me as I study His word. Without His grace, His love, His forgiveness and His steadfastness we can't stay the course because the guilt will sink in to deep and pull us down.

I pray that when the doubts, fears and grumblings begin in our hearts, our minds quickly turn to all the moments and miracles God has allowed us to join him in.

Not Yet! . . . . Just another minute

Then the LORD said to me, "You have made your way around this hill country long enough; now turn north. Give the people these orders: 'You are about to pass through the territory of your relatives the descendants of Esau, who live in Seir. They will be afraid of you, but be very careful. Do not provoke them to war, for I will not give you any of their land, not even enough to put your foot on. I have given Esau the hill country of Seir as his own." Deuteronomy 2:2-5

As I think back on all the times I acted before the Lord was ready for me to (or before I consulted Him) I cringe. Yikes! I can promise you this, all those moments turned out as either failures, delays or destruction.

38

None of which are my favorite things to encounter in life. I believe this is why it seemed as if a floodlight was shining brightly on these verses.

Finally, God tells Moses they have wandered around the desert long enough and it's time to get moving a start taking over some land. "Turn north!" the Lord tells him, but when you pass through this land don't even think about taking it. The Lord tells Moses they won't get enough of this land to even put their foot on so keep moving! In other words, don't waste your time. Thankfully, Moses was a great listener when it came to the Lord, not to mention a great advocate for his wayward Israelites. As they continue, the Lord faithfully gives Moses clear instructions on what to do as they travel through each bit of land.

The LORD said to me, "Today you are to pass by the region of Moab at Ar. When you come to the Ammonites, do not harass them or provoke them to war, for I will not give you possession of any land belonging to the Ammonites. I have given it as a possession to the descendants of Lot." Deuteronomy 2:17-19

Surely, after all those years of wandering the desert, the Israelites are more than excited to begin claiming some land for themselves. Settling down would have been their greatest desire at this point. I think that's why I find it so amazing they listened to God as they went even He said, "No, not yet, not this piece of land, just a few more miles … OK, now!"

"Set out now and cross the Arnon Gorge. See, I have given into your hand Sihon the Amorite, king of Heshbon, and his country. Begin to take possession of it and engage him in battle. This very day I will begin to put the terror and fear of you on all the nations under heaven. They will hear reports of you and will tremble and be in anguish because of you." Deuteronomy 2:24-25

And finally, they received the instructions they had been waiting for years and years to hear and began to take the land that **"God handed over to them" (v.33).** What if we lived like this? Heck, what if we listened like this? What if we never acted until God showed us the correct path? We wouldn't wander and find defeat, delay or destruction by taking matters into our own hands because we got tired of waiting. What if we listened and trusted God's plan, and as a result, our actions produced success, built up the Kingdom of God and the outcomes were never hindered by selfish desires? Just considering it makes me marvel at what this world could look like if we could all live a little more like this.

Are you waiting to hear from the Lord? Are you considering taking matters into your own hands because He doesn't seem to be listening or answering in your time frame? Will you join me as I pray for myself and all of us who struggle with the desire to get things crossed of the list, to conquer or to consider ourselves before others? I pray we can all be a little more like Moses in the wait.

  Notes and Reflections:

Week 11

- ☐ Monday - Deuteronomy 3-4
- ☐ Tuesday - Deuteronomy 5-7
- ☐ Wednesday - Deuteronomy 8-10
- ☐ Thursday - Deuteronomy 11-13
- ☐ Friday - Deuteronomy 14-16
- ☐ Saturday - Deuteronomy 17-20
- ☐ Sunday - Deuteronomy 21-23

Week 12

- ☐ Monday - Deuteronomy 24-27
- ☐ Tuesday - Deuteronomy 28-29
- ☐ Wednesday - Deuteronomy 30-31
- ☐ Thursday - Deuteronomy 32-34; Psalm 91
- ☐ Friday - Joshua 1-4
- ☐ Saturday – Joshua 5-8
- ☐ Sunday – Joshua 9-11

Revelations	
Questions	
Repeats	
Deeper Study	
Etc.	

Seeking Shelter?

Whoever dwells in the shelter of the Most High will rest in the shadow of the Almighty. ² I will say of the LORD, "He is my refuge and my fortress, my God, in whom I trust." Psalm 91:1-2

Today will be short and sweet, but I pray a powerful reminder of the God we serve and the provision He promises those who seek and obey Him. So often, Satan will try to bind our hearts and minds with lies of shame, fear, distrust, guilt, anger and desires for us to feel all alone in our struggles, temptations and lives. When we are isolated, the lies grow louder and louder. They overcome and overwhelm us leaving us with a feeling of defeat.

Satan strives to make us feel alone and vulnerable. He wants us to think we aren't good enough so that we don't have the courage to move forward from the past and climb out of the pit, but our God is cheering for us!

Resist him, standing firm in the faith, because you know that the family of believers throughout the world is undergoing the same kind of sufferings. 1 Peter 5:9

David penned **Psalm 91** after Saul pursued him and promised him death, but God prevailed and opened Saul's eyes through David's noble decision not to harm or disgrace Saul (1 Samuel 24). David is giving praise to God for delivering him from his enemy (Saul). In these verses are some amazing reminders of the protection God promises if we are dwelling and abiding in Him.

Verse 4 – putting us under His wing

Verse 5 – gives us confidence so we will not fear

Verse 11 – promises us assistance from His angels

Verse 14 – promises to rescue and protect us if we love Him

While God doesn't promise to remove us from the battle or the conflict, he does promise protection if we are dwelling in Him. But how? Where do we start? How do we make it happen? Over and over again He tells us to simply ask.

Call to me and I will answer you and tell you great and unsearchable things you do not know. Jeremiah 33:3

"So I say to you: Ask and it will be given to you; seek and you will find; knock and the door will be opened to you." Luke 11:9

If any of you lacks wisdom, he should ask God, who gives generously to all without finding fault, and it will be given to him. James 1:5

What should we do if we need wisdom, faith, healing, peace, courage, discipline? Ask! Just ask. There is no special form and no fee, just ask with a willing heart.

Read Psalm 91 in its entirety below and each word and promise soak in to your heart today.

   Notes and Reflections:

Week 13

- ☐ Monday - Joshua 12-15
- ☐ Tuesday - Joshua 16-18
- ☐ Wednesday - Joshua 19-21
- ☐ Thursday - Joshua 22-24
- ☐ Friday - Judges 1-2
- ☐ Saturday - Judges 3-5
- ☐ Sunday - Judges 6-7

Week 14

- ☐ Monday - Judges 8-9
- ☐ Tuesday - Judges 10-12
- ☐ Wednesday - Judges 13-15
- ☐ Thursday - Judges 16-18
- ☐ Friday - Judges 19-21
- ☐ Saturday - Ruth 1-4
- ☐ Sunday - 1 Samuel 1-3

Revelations	
Questions	
Repeats	
Deeper Study	
Etc.	

Picnic with an Angel

Many times people have asked me, "Why don't we see angels anymore? They talk about Angels coming to share a message from the Lord with someone often in the Bible. Do they still come?" As I read through Judges, something struck me about the visits from the angels of the Lord. When they arrived to speak to the people, they had no idea until sometime later that they were even angels. Let's look at two specific angel appearances. First, let's look at the angel that comes to visit Gideon whom I wrote about last week. He was chosen by God to free the Israelites from Midian after being under their control for seven years.

Read Judges 6:11-14.

I love how the Angel of the Lord just takes a seat under the oak tree and waits for Gideon to come by. No bright lights or fancy entry here. In fact, what's amazing is that is isn't until after a conversation and when he returns to bring an offering of meat and bread that the realization he has been speaking to an angel hits him. Then . . . **the angel of the LORD touched the meat and the unleavened bread with the tip of the staff that was in his hand. Fire flared from the rock, consuming the meat and the bread. And the angel of the LORD disappeared. When Gideon realized that it was the angel of the LORD, he exclaimed, "Alas, Sovereign LORD! I have seen the angel of the LORD face to face!" Judges 6:21-22**

Later in Judges, we meet Manoah and his wife who learn from a "man of God" that after years of not being able to conceive she finally will. The angel gives her very specific instructions (Judges 13:3-5) including they are to never cut the child's hair and he (Samson) will have favor with God and save Israel from the Philistines. She tells her husband

47

and he prays God will send the man again so he can hear the news for himself. God answers and Manoah meets the man, hears the news of a coming baby with his own ears and in gratitude he offers to prepare a young goat for him.

The angel of the LORD replied, "Even though you detain me, I will not eat any of your food. But if you prepare a burnt offering, offer it to the LORD." (Manoah did not realize that it was the angel of the LORD.) Then Manoah inquired of the angel of the LORD, "What is your name, so that we may honor you when your word comes true?" He replied, "Why do you ask my name? It is beyond understanding." Then Manoah took a young goat, together with the grain offering, and sacrificed it on a rock to the LORD. And the LORD did an amazing thing while Manoah and his wife watched: As the flame blazed up from the altar toward heaven, the angel of the LORD ascended in the flame. Seeing this, Manoah and his wife fell with their faces to the ground. Judges 13:16-20

Yes, both angel encounters ended with an amazing feat that made it very clear the angels were sent from the Lord. However, until that occurred Gideon, Manoah and his wife had no idea they were in the presence of angels. It makes me think: they must have looked very normal, average and humanlike for them not to suspect anything until that miraculous moment of realization. If that's the case, then couldn't we still be in the presence of angels now, just as God's people were then? Just because we don't get the miraculous signs doesn't mean they don't walk among us. With all the noise and business of this world, I can see how we would even miss the miraculous if it were there. I would like to think the angels do walk among us daily. Either way, we have the Holy Spirit within each of us when we accept Christ. We are never without our God of angel armies.

Week 15

- ☐ Monday - 1 Samuel 4-8
- ☐ Tuesday - 1 Samuel 9-12
- ☐ Wednesday - 1 Samuel 13-14
- ☐ Thursday - 1 Samuel 15-17
- ☐ Friday - 1 Samuel 18-20; Psalm 11, 59
- ☐ Saturday - 1 Samuel 21-24
- ☐ Sunday - Psalm 7, 27, 31, 34, 52

Week 16

- ☐ Monday - Psalm 56, 120, 140-142
- ☐ Tuesday - 1 Samuel 25-27
- ☐ Wednesday - Psalm 17, 35, 54, 63
- ☐ Thursday - 1 Samuel 28-31; Psalm 18
- ☐ Friday - Psalm 121, 123-125, 128-130
- ☐ Saturday - 2 Samuel 1-4
- ☐ Sunday - Psalm 6, 8-10, 14, 16, 19, 21

Revelations	
Questions	
Repeats	
Deeper Study	
Etc.	

I "Heart" This Reminder

As Samuel began to phase out of his leadership, God revealed that Saul would take over and lead the Israelites as their first King. During this time of transition, Samuel shares with his people a great reminder:

"Do not be afraid," Samuel replied. "You have done all this evil; yet do not turn away from the LORD, but serve the LORD with all your heart. Do not turn away to follow after useless idols. They can do you no good, nor can they rescue you, because they are useless. For the sake of his great name the LORD will not reject his people, because the LORD was pleased to make you his own. As for me, far be it from me that I should sin against the LORD by failing to pray for you. And I will teach you the way that is good and right. But be sure to fear the LORD and serve him faithfully with all your heart; consider what great things he has done for you. 1 Samuel 12:20-24

These words especially hit home for me today after a close friend confided in me about a very challenging and sinful situation their child was involved in. As we talked and prayed together, I was reminded of the times in my life I strayed from God and lived in a rebellious state through a sinful nature. Maybe you can relate, too. During these times we can be afraid God won't forgive us, that we have gone too far this time, that our sin is too big to start over. We turn to idols of busyness, greed, success, fear, materialism, alcoholism, retail therapy … pick your poison.

But, no sin is ever too big for God to conquer if we allow Him into our lives and hearts to do His work. It's never too late to turn away from useless idols and turn back to God. He is always there waiting for our return so He can restore us, heal us and make us whole again. Look at these great reminders we can pull from Samuel's message to the Israelites and use in our lives today:

51

- Do not be afraid

- You have done evil things, but don't turn God away

- Serve God with all your heart

- Turn away from useless idols that can't rescue you

- God will not reject you, you are His child

- Consider all the great things God has done for you and serve Him with a faithful heart

If I could tell my children, friends and others just a few things, it would be these truths Samuel spoke so long ago. When we consider what our lives would look if we followed this wise advice, it's overwhelming. It seems too simple to be effective or real. The challenge is putting faith into action and holding onto God's provision and promises. I'm praying with God's strength we all begin to live our lives in the way Samuel encouraged the Israelites to live thousands of years ago.

David Rocks!

David rocks, literally (pun intended)! As we continue in 1 Samuel we see how Saul, appointed to lead the Israelites, makes some disappointing choices and goes against God's commands. This causes God to withdraw His anointing from Saul, and he has Samuel anoint David as the future leader of His people. David has a long and arduous journey to the throne. I will write about that more in the upcoming weeks, but today I want to talk about that old story most of us have heard a hundred times growing up in the church: the story of David and Goliath.

As I read these verses again something new stood out to me. First, David was met with great doubt by those around him. His brothers and

King Saul all quickly reminded him that he was only a young boy with no experience (1 Sam. 17:33). However, this had no effect on the faith and trust he had in God saying, "The Lord who rescued me from the paw of the lion and the paw of the bear will rescue me from the hand of this Philistine" (v. 37). Even Goliath (the Philistine) looked at David and "despised him because he was just a youth, healthy and handsome" (v. 42).

Clearly David was one with total confidence and trust in God. He boldly stood up to Goliath, who was 9' 9" tall with armor weighing 125 pounds, when no one else would (1 Sam. 17:5). Not only did David take on Goliath, he took him on with absolutely no armor and only a slingshot and five smooth stones instead of a sword.

David said to the Philistine, "You come against me with sword and spear and javelin, but I come against you in the name of the Lord Almighty, the God of the armies of Israel, whom you have defied (v.35).

Again, just like God did with Moses, he set the stage for the miraculous to happen, so there was no denying that His hand is upon David and the Israelite people. It wasn't even a close battle. As we know, David slings that first rock and lays Goliath out, only then taking the sword to remove his head.

A sling and a stone held by a boy took out a giant. That's the God we serve! He doesn't need us to conquer the giants, He only needs a willing heart that trusts He will show up and conquer the giant through us with His strength and might. What is the giant you are facing today? Maybe you have placed yourself before the giant, or maybe you have found yourself standing before one by no choice of your own. Whatever the case may be, will you trust that the mighty God we serve can take it down for you, with only a sling and a stone, through your trust in Him?

 Notes and Reflections:

Week 17

- ☐ Monday - 1 Chronicles 1-2
- ☐ Tuesday - Psalm 43-45, 49, 84-85, 87
- ☐ Wednesday - 1 Chronicles 3-5
- ☐ Thursday - Psalm 73, 77-78
- ☐ Friday - 1 Chronicles 6
- ☐ Saturday - Psalm 81, 88, 92-93
- ☐ Sunday - 1 Chronicles 7-10

Week 18

- ☐ Monday - Psalm 102-104
- ☐ Tuesday - 2 Samuel 5:1-10; 1 Chronicles 11-12
- ☐ Wednesday - Psalm 133
- ☐ Thursday - Psalm 106-107
- ☐ Friday - 2 Samuel 5:11-25; 2 Samuel 6:1-23; 1 Chronicles 13-16
- ☐ Saturday - Psalm 1-2, 15, 22-24, 47, 68
- ☐ Sunday - Psalm 89, 96, 100, 101, 105, 132

Revelations	
Questions	
Repeats	
Deeper Study	
Etc.	

Unseen Footprints

These verses from Psalm 77:16-20 that David penned as he reflected on God's provision and promise keeping for his people stirred my heart as I read them.

The waters saw you, God, the waters saw you and writhed; the very depths were convulsed. The clouds poured down water, the heavens resounded with thunder; your arrows flashed back and forth. Your thunder was heard in the whirlwind, your lightning lit up the world; the earth trembled and quaked. Your path led through the sea, your way through the mighty waters, though your footprints were not seen. You led your people like a flock by the hand of Moses and Aaron.

There have been many times in my life that the storm waters seemed to rise faster than I can escape to higher ground. Fearing sorrow, pain or disappointment will overtake me, I sometimes swim so fast I miss God's face. Things move so quickly and my mind is so cluttered in times of crisis, God can sometimes seem like nothing more than a blur. "Where are you in all of this? How can this suffering be made into a thing of beauty?" I cry out.

In those times, I try to remind myself that I am only human. Knowing and trusting that God will prevail, allowing me to rise from the ashes and make something spectacular out of the horrible is what gets me through. I've seen it happen. I've seen Him work in truly astonishing ways. When I have the moments that I cry out wondering why His "footprints are unseen" I stop. I look. I listen. I trust. And unfortunately this isn't normally easy.

In the midst of wild storms and trials our God is always there, but don't forget to stop and take note of your surroundings. Somewhere among you He has sent someone to lead, love and guide you, just as David reminds us God did for the Israelites through the leadership of Moses and Aaron. So, don't forget to look around next time you are in a storm. Look around and you will no doubt discover a life-preserver floating nearby that you need only trust and grab onto. You may not see Him, but He is there and you will sense Him if you stop for a moment in stillness.

And when you aren't in a storm? Please continue to look for Him, because there is always a storm brewing somewhere and you never know who God will place in your path that may need you to throw out a life-preserver to.

Although we may not see His footsteps clearly, He truly is in every detail.

I will give thanks to you, LORD, with all my heart; I will tell of all your wonderful deeds. I will be glad and rejoice in you; I will sing the praises of your name, O Most High. Psalm 9:1-2

With ALL Your Might?

Ever felt as if your love for others is seen as a weakness, your joy in the midst of trial as ignorance, your peace in the fury viewed suspicious, your kindness as flirting, or your zealous praise for our God and Savior unusual? As Christians, these characteristics are common when we trust and rely on God for strength, peace and direction, but those who aren't

Christ followers can easily misinterpret them because they don't understand the power of faith and God's love.

In 2 Samuel 6:14-16, we find David rejoicing as the Ark of the Lord returns to the city of David to finally be placed inside the tent David prepared for it. In verse 14 it says, **"David was dancing with all his might before the LORD wearing a linen ephod."** I love to imagine what someone dancing with "all of their might" looks like. It reminds me of a video I shared years ago of my son on the beach doing his happy dance.

In 1 Chronicles 15:28 it even tells us that, **"All Israel brought up the ark of the covenant of the LORD with shouts, the sound of the ram's horn, trumpets and cymbals, and the playing of harps and lyres."** What a celebration it must have been to finally have the ark of the Lord among them once again. However, when you continue in the verses, you see that one of David's wives (Saul's daughter, Michal), **"looked down from the window and saw King David leaping and dancing before the LORD, and she despised him in her heart" (v.29).**

There are a few different reasons that scholars believe Michal looked upon David in disgust. First, she may have been angry that, when David returned after Saul's death to lead Israel, he had Michal taken from her second husband and returned to him (since Saul gave David Michal in marriage years earlier). Second, she may have seen his behavior as vulgar as she states in the verses below.

When David returned home to bless his household, Michal daughter of Saul came out to meet him and said, "How the king of Israel has distinguished himself today, going around half-naked in full view of the slave girls of his servants as any vulgar fellow would!" (v. 29)

However, another reason given for her disgust is that she was may not have had a sincere faith in God. We see in 1 Samuel 19:13, **"Then Michal took the household idol and put it on the bed, placed some goat hair on its head, and covered it with a garment."**

The latter had more to do with Michal's disgust at David's praise explosion than anything else. So often when we are judged for our faith, confidence and trust in God it's by others who do not share the same level of faith that we do. We understand God's hand is in every detail and try to confidently live in His divine plan. However, those who do not have a strong faith, or any faith at all, may see it as a weakness, vulnerability or just simply not understand so they find it odd. I believe that is where Michal was. She may have even had a bit of jealously in her heart for the love and faith David had in God. All that said, never be discouraged when you are judged, for you are in good company. Get out there and trust with all your might, praise with all your might, believe with all your might and show off your faith with all of your might.

David said to Michal, "It was before the LORD, who chose me rather than your father or anyone from his house when he appointed me ruler over the LORD's people Israel—I will celebrate before the LORD. I will become even more undignified than this, and I will be humiliated in my own eyes. But by these slave girls you spoke of, I will be held in honor." And Michal daughter of Saul had no children to the day of her death. 2 Samuel 6:21-23

 Notes and Reflections:

Week 19

- ☐ Monday - 2 Samuel 7; 1 Chronicles 17
- ☐ Tuesday - Psalm 25, 29, 33, 36, 39
- ☐ Wednesday - 2 Samuel 8-9; 1 Chronicles 18
- ☐ Thursday - Psalm 50, 53, 60, 75
- ☐ Friday - 2 Samuel 10; 1 Chronicles 19; Psalm 20
- ☐ Saturday - Psalm 65-67, 69-70
- ☐ Sunday - 2 Samuel 11-12; 1 Chronicles 20

Week 20

- ☐ Monday - Psalm 32, 51, 86, 122
- ☐ Tuesday - 2 Samuel 13-15
- ☐ Wednesday - Psalm 3-4, 12-13, 28, 55
- ☐ Thursday - 2 Samuel 16-18
- ☐ Friday - Psalm 26, 40, 58, 61-62, 64
- ☐ Saturday - 2 Samuel 19-21
- ☐ Sunday - Psalm 5, 38, 41-42

Revelations	
Questions	
Repeats	
Deeper Study	
Etc.	

The Ripple Effect

In 2 Samuel 11-12, we find David at home wandering around his palace when he should have been off at war with his men. **"In the spring when kings march out to war, David sent Joab with his officers all Israel. They destroyed the Ammonites and besieged Rabbah, but David remained in Jerusalem." 2 Samuel 11:1**

I have often wondered why David decided to stay during that time when kings usually accompanied their soldiers. Was he sick, injured, depressed or had he spotted Bathsheba before and wanted everyone to be at war when he made his move? In any case, he remained and spotted Bathsheba, a married woman, from his balcony and sent for her. He blatantly disobeyed God by having sex with a married woman and committing adultery.

After all we read about God doing for David in previous chapters, it's difficult to understand how David could have turned so abruptly. Or is it? Don't we do it daily? Maybe not with an "in your face" offense like adultery, but with idols of greed, coveting and gossip. After all God had done for David, he blew it in one moment of weakness. We are familiar with the story of sin, but I want to focus on the response from God.

At this point in 2 Samuel, David is hearing from God through the prophet Nathan. Nathan reminds David of all God blessed him with, protected him, from and has promised him and then drops the sentence. **"I am going to bring disaster on you from your own family: I will take your wives and give them to another before your very eyes, and he will sleep with them publicly. You acted in secret, but I will do this before all Israel and in broad daylight." 2 Samuel 12:11-12**

David responded to Nathan, **"I have sinned against the LORD." Then Nathan replied to David, "The LORD has taken away your sin; you will not die. However, because you treated the LORD with such contempt in this matter, the son born to you (and Bathsheba) will die." 2 Samuel 12:13-14**

God had already promised David (2 Samuel 7:15-16) that He would not remove His faithful love from David as He had done to Saul and that his kingdom would be established forever. Nathan even tells David that he will not die and his sins have been taken away. However, we see the consequences of his sin do not go away. Nathan explains to David that his son will die and disaster will fall on his family. We become disillusioned if we believe that being forgiven for our sins means that everything will go back to normal. That there will be no consequences. That our entire slate is wiped clean and we start fresh. We do start fresh when it comes to forgiveness in God's eyes. We are wiped clean and white again with the blood of His sacrifice each time we repent, but repenting does not mean that the consequences of our actions are erased or go away. The ripple effect continues, but it doesn't mean God hasn't forgiven you. I have fallen prey to Satan's lies in the past because, when I repented, the consequences of my sins continued on.

This is where the rubber meets the road in our faith. We must remember that each time we sin and humbly repent God is quick to forgive, but that the ripples sin creates can't be stopped. Do not confuse consequences with unforgiveness. The forgiveness remains even as the consequences continue on.

There's A Psalm for That

One of the greatest things about reading the Bible in chronological order for me so far is that mixed in Chronicles and 1 & 2 Samuel (David's story) are the Psalms he wrote. They are placed in proper sequence so that you read the Psalm in direct response to his current circumstances. As we meandered through his rise to kingship and fall to sin, Psalm 86 caught my eye.

On those days when you aren't sure what to pray, you are overcome with grief, busyness, your circumstances and you can't think straight but need to be on your knees talking to God, this is just what we need. Psalm 86, called David's Prayer, is a diamond in the rough and covers almost all we need from the Lord on a daily basis. I call it my "God, please" prayer.

Take a look at what David asks of the Lord and see how much it relates to what we need ourselves.

God, please . . .answer me (v.1), protect my life (v.2), be gracious to me (v.3), bring joy to my life (v. 4), make me rich in faithful love (v. 5), listen to my plea (v.6), answer me (v.7), teach me your way (v.11), give me an undivided mind to fear your name (v.11), turn to me and be gracious to me (v. 16), give me your strength (v.16), show me a sign of your goodness, help and comfort me (v.17).

My pen and heart went crazy as I read this Psalm. There have been so many times in my life when my heart and mind have been paralyzed from grief, sadness and despair. So much so, that I wasn't able to pray as I felt I needed to; and here it is, right here in Psalms written out perfectly. All the provisions and things we desire from the Lord to equip us with and all we crave to receive from Him. So, next time you are in need of a little prayer direction, look to the Psalms. For David surely experienced almost every emotion, circumstance and sin we could imagine and has a prayer for that!

Reread and rest in the words of Psalm 86 for a few moments.

Sticks and Stones

Shame and guilt can be like ugly warts that won't go away. They appear, begin to grow quickly and are difficult to get rid of. So often we don't want to face the fallout of our actions, so we remove ourselves from the situation entirely, hoping that the memories will fade and take the shame and guilt with it. That's why as I read 2 Samuel 16, it tugged at my heart. In this chapter, we find King David running from his son Absalom who conspired to overthrow him. Fleeing quickly, David reaches a town where he ran into Shimei, a man from the house of Saul.

He pelted David and all the king's officials with stones, though all the troops and the special guard were on David's right and left. As he cursed, Shimei said, "Get out, get out, you murderer, you scoundrel! The LORD has repaid you for all the blood you shed in the household of Saul, in whose place you have reigned. The LORD has given the kingdom into the hands of your son Absalom. You have come to ruin because you are a murderer!" 2 Samuel 16:6-8

I don't know about you, but I struggle enough with past sins without someone screaming them out in public at me as I walk by. Quickly, David's loyal companion defends him and offers to cut off Shimei's head to stop the cursing. However, David's response is what caught my attention.

But the king said, "What does this have to do with you, you sons of Zeruiah? If he is cursing because the LORD said to him, 'Curse David,' who can ask, 'Why do you do this?'"

David then said to Abishai and all his officials, "My son, my own flesh and blood, is trying to kill me. How much more, then, this Benjamite! Leave him alone; let him curse, for the LORD has told him to. It may be that the LORD will look upon my misery and restore to me his covenant blessing instead of his curse today."

So David and his men continued along the road while Shimei was going along the hillside opposite him, cursing as he went and throwing stones at him and showering him with dirt. The king and all the people with him arrived at their destination exhausted. And there he refreshed himself. 2 Samuel 16:10-14

David defends Shimei and tells his men to allow him to continue cursing him. No secret service action needed. David understood he deserved this and no matter how difficult and shameful it must have been, he allowed it to continue for miles as they traveled and Shimei followed them. Not only cursing at David, but throwing stones and dirt on him. Talk about free speech.

David was hopeful that if he allowed Shimei to follow the Lord's instructions to curse David, that the Lord might look upon him with pity and bless David once again (v.12). David was strong enough to take the sticks and stones he had earned by sinning so grievously against God when he slept with Bathsheba and had her husband murdered. He understood he was paying the price for those sins and that God wasn't

67

finished with him yet. He didn't allow shame and guilt to overwhelm and overcome the lesson he desired to learn from his past mistakes. He realized there were consequences, admitted his mistakes, took the condemnation but kept moving forward. With hope as his anchor, he kept following God and trusting He would restore His covenant with him once again.

I have such adoration for the amount of trust and faith David had that God was still with Him, that He would eventually restore him and that God would not forsake him. So often in the heat of the battle the lights grow dim on hope, faith and trust because they are overshadowed by the guilt and shame. Let's put it all out there in the light just like David, cleansing our hearts daily, turning it all over to God and trusting in the restoration He desires for us.

Keep moving forward! We may end up dirty and bruised when we arrive at our destination, but God will restore, renew and refresh us when we arrive.

 Notes and Reflections:

Week 21

- [ ] Monday - 2 Samuel 22-23; Psalm 57
- [ ] Tuesday - Psalm 95, 97-99
- [ ] Wednesday - 2 Samuel 24; 1 Chronicles 21-22; Psalm 30
- [ ] Thursday - Psalm 108-110
- [ ] Friday - 1 Chronicles 23-25
- [ ] Saturday - Psalm 131, 138-139, 143-145
- [ ] Sunday - 1 Chronicles 26-29; Psalm 127

Week 22

- [ ] Monday - Psalm 111-118
- [ ] Tuesday - 1 Kings 1-2; Psalm 37, 71, 94
- [ ] Wednesday - Psalm 119:1-88
- [ ] Thursday - 1 Kings 3-4; 2 Chronicles 1; Psalm 72
- [ ] Friday - Psalm 119:89-176
- [ ] Saturday - Song of Solomon 1-8
- [ ] Sunday - Proverbs 1-3

Revelations	
Questions	
Repeats	
Deeper Study	
Etc.	

The Numbers Game

We have been following the life and adventures of David over the past few weeks. This week we find Absalom (David's son, who tried to overthrow him) has died in battle and David restored to the throne once again. Then something interesting occurs. David gets caught up in a little social media addiction. Well, something like that. Let's take a look.

Satan rose up against Israel and incited David to take a census of Israel. So David said to Joab and the commanders of the troops, "Go and count the Israelites from Beersheba to Dan. Then report back to me so that I may know how many there are." 1 Chronicles 21:1-2

Out of the blue, Satan decides to stick his ugly claws into David once again, and he decides to count all the people under his control. When I first read this, I wasn't sure what the big deal was. Why shouldn't a king take a census of his people? However, David must have forgotten God's stipulation for taking a census. **"When you take a census of the Israelites to register them, each of the men must pay a ransom for himself to the LORD as they are registered. Then no plague will come on them as they are registered" (Exodus 30:12).**

Since David didn't take up any ransom, he was only interested in the numbers. This need to count stemmed from David's own pride and the desire to see how many people were under his thumb. It reminds me of when my children post a picture to Instagram and continue to look back to see how many people have "liked" it or when they compare how many followers they each have. Apparently, there is even an unspoken rule that, if you don't have a certain number of "likes" on a picture, you should delete it off your account entirely because it's not worth keeping if enough people don't like it. I'm not sure what is scarier: letting others decide what things in your life are worth

71

remembering or having your self-worth being tied up into how many followers you have on your social media accounts. Either way, it didn't turn out well for David in his situation.

This command was also evil in the sight of God; so he punished Israel. Then David said to God, "I have sinned greatly by doing this. Now, I beg you, take away the guilt of your servant. I have done a very foolish thing." The LORD said to Gad, David's seer, "Go and tell David, 'This is what the LORD says: I am giving you three options. Choose one of them for me to carry out against you.'" 1 Chronicles 21:7-9

David's prideful decision wasn't going to vanish. He had to decide if he wanted three years of famine, three months of devastation by his foes, or a plague to cover the land. Maybe if we had punishments like that when pride took over, we would try to stifle it more and find our strength, beauty and self-worth only in God. Maybe?

The Inexperienced

The LORD is gracious and righteous; our God is compassionate. The LORD guards the inexperienced; I was helpless, and He saved me. Return to your rest, my soul, for the LORD has been good to you. Psalm 116:5-7

As I read Psalm 116, the word "inexperienced" caught my eye. The Holman Study Bible says that the inexperienced "are naïve people, usually young who are uncommitted, they lack common sense and prefer folly over wisdom" (pg. 1031). I feel as though I am living proof of these words David lived out and penned so long ago. Without a doubt, I know that the Lord does, indeed, guard the inexperienced. In my young adult life I believed I was a true Christian, but was so inexperienced, so naïve, selfish, so willing to sit on the fence instead of take a stand for Jesus.

In short, I was helpless. Thank goodness God saved me. After looking for love in all the wrong places, using business and partying to keep my mind off past and present sin, and being chained by the guilt and shame that comes along with all that sin, God saved me. As I began to read and study His written word, He came alive to me for the first time. I no longer sat on the sidelines and allowed others to tell me about God. I got to know Him for myself. After a few years of that, there was no turning back. God busted through every chain that had bound me and put my soul at rest. Be careful not to misinterpret those words. My heart has cried out, been broken by sadness, overcome with fear, doubt and anger at times in the journey, but my soul … my soul rests in God. He saved me and continues to save me every single day (and sometimes every hour of every day).

Are you feeling inexperienced? Like you need a little saving? Please dive into His word. While Bible study tools written by others such as this one are great places to start, there is no substitute for getting into the Bible and reading God's word for yourself.* The Bible sitting on your shelf is the living, breathing word of God. He is waiting for you to pick it up and discover His mysteries of forgiveness, love, grace, compassion and provision. I promise it's there. All those things. They are there. His Word will give you understanding (Psalm 119:130), teach you to be shrewd (Proverbs 8:5) and most of all help you leave inexperience behind (Proverbs 9:6). I have savored the mysteries and promises of His word and cling to them in every aspect of my life. Will you run to Him, cling to Him and allow Him to save you, redeem you and bring rest to your soul?

The proverbs of Solomon son of David, king of Israel: For learning what wisdom and discipline are; for understanding insightful sayings; for receiving wise instruction in righteousness, justice, and integrity; for teaching shrewdness to the inexperienced, knowledge and discretion to a young man— Proverbs 1:1-4

*If you are looking for a good Bible study on how to study the Bible on your own that is relevant and doable please check out In the Mi[God]dle.

Seeking What?

if you seek it [wisdom] like silver and search for it like hidden treasure, then you will understand the fear of the LORD and discover the knowledge of God. For the LORD gives wisdom; from His mouth come knowledge and understanding. Proverbs 2:4-6

Throughout Proverbs, Solomon speaks of wisdom. Reminding us often that we are to seek wisdom only from God and not ourselves (Proverbs 3) and that we should hold onto wisdom tightly and guard it (Proverbs 4:13). I wonder how our lives would look if we sought out God's wisdom like we do fortune, approval from others, high paying salaries or the newest toys. So often, in our flesh, we seek things such as happiness, contentment, more money, financial security, pleasure and wisdom from the wrong source. How often do we go to God who is the ultimate and only provider of perfect discoveries, contentment, security and wisdom? We tend to skip God altogether and seek these things through our own doing and by the world's guidance.

Solomon describes wisdom in two very unique ways in chapters seven and nine of Proverbs. First, we see him describe wisdom as a sister.

74

Say to wisdom, "You are my sister," and call understanding your relative. ⁵ She will keep you from a forbidden woman, a stranger with her flattering talk. Proverbs 7:4-5

In other words, keep wisdom as close as your sibling (or as close as God intended siblings to be). When you do this, wisdom will keep you from making foolish mistakes like adultery, as Proverbs 7 goes on to explain. Solomon also describes wisdom as a house with seven pillars. Seven being the number of perfection, so we should say, "the perfect house."

Read Proverbs 9:1-6.

Wisdom is inviting you to attend a feast in her perfect home. The table is set and she is calling to you to enter and leave all "inexperience" behind so that you can pursue understanding. What a beautiful image. Will you leave behind inexperience today and chart a new course towards gaining wisdom and understanding of God's word and will for you? He has so much to offer if only we would enter and sit at the table before Him with our hearts open and ready to receive. Will you seek Him and trust in His provision?

 Notes and Reflections:

Week 23

- ☐ Monday - Proverbs 4-6
- ☐ Tuesday - Proverbs 7-9
- ☐ Wednesday - Proverbs 10-12
- ☐ Thursday - Proverbs 13-15
- ☐ Friday - Proverbs 16-18
- ☐ Saturday - Proverbs 19-21
- ☐ Sunday - Proverbs 22-24

Week 24

- ☐ Monday - 1 Kings 5-6; 2 Chronicles 2-3
- ☐ Tuesday - 1 Kings 7; 2 Chronicles 4
- ☐ Wednesday - 1 Kings 8; 2 Chronicles 5
- ☐ Thursday - 2 Chronicles 6-7; Psalm 136
- ☐ Friday - Psalm 134, 146-150
- ☐ Saturday - 1 Kings 9; 2 Chronicles 8
- ☐ Sunday - Proverbs 25-26

Revelations	
Questions	
Repeats	
Deeper Study	
Etc.	

Pomegranates

I love pomegranates. They are a bear to peel, extract the seeds and enjoy, but worth the effort to keep cool and nibble on throughout the day. If you have never tasted the fresh plump seeds inside, put it on this week's grocery list and give it a try. So what does this have to do with the Bible?

Well, as I read over and over again in 1 Kings 7-8 how Solomon had the pomegranate etched in the pillars of the temple, I wondered more about this strange fruit. Around 200 pomegranates were etched here and 400 there within the walls, and I began to ponder the significance of the pomegranate to King Solomon and the Israelites as they rebuilt God's great temple in Jerusalem.

Back in Exodus 28:33-34 it says, **"Make pomegranates of blue, purple, and scarlet yarn on its lower hem and all around it. Put gold bells between them all the way around, so that gold bells and pomegranates alternate around the lower hem of the robe."**

And in 2 Chronicles 3:16, **"He had made chainwork in the inner sanctuary and also put it on top of the pillars. He made 100 pomegranates and fastened them into the chainwork"**

Who knew? This is the beauty of God's word. It breathes, it offers wisdom and new insights each time we read it. It never grows stale, weary or out of date. Within the text, we discover the pomegranate has great significance in the Jewish tradition or it certainly would not have been all over holy places. Many scholars even believe the pomegranate was the "forbidden fruit" that Adam and Eve gave into while in the Garden of Eden. Not only that, like many others things in the Bible,

78

there is a numerical symbolism as well. Jewish tradition says that this amazing fruit is a symbol of righteousness because, like the 613 commandments of the Torah (the law of God as revealed to Moses and recorded in the first five books of the Hebrew scriptures), the pomegranate also has 613 seeds. Now, I've never taken the time to count this for myself. I'm just going with what most scholars say and trusting in those Jewish scholars.

Because of all those seeds, the pomegranate also represents knowledge, fruitfulness, fertility and wisdom. Its healing effects are also believed to help remedy and aid in many, illnesses including prostate cancer, infant brain injury and male infertility. In Song of Solomon it is the pomegranate fields where he wants to proclaim his love.

Let's go early to the vineyards; let's see if the vine has budded, if the blossom has opened, if the pomegranates are in bloom. There I will give you my love. Song of Solomon 7:12

In Deuteronomy 8:7-8 we see this lush fruit is one of the delicacies found in the promised land after the Israelites' desert wanderings are complete.

For the LORD your God is bringing you into a good land, a land with streams of water, springs, and deep water sources, flowing in both valleys and hills; a land of wheat, barley, vines, figs, and pomegranates; a land of olive oil and honey.

So, yes! Pomegranates were very important and symbolic fruit. This is one of the great ways to study and dig deeper into scripture as you read it. Notice repetition, what seems unusual to you or stands out, dig deeper, discover and unlock the deeper meaning so that God's word can come alive in and stay rooted in your heart. As you seek to understand His ways and the mysteries of His word, He becomes more alive and real to you. I pray you begin to thirst for Him in ways you never imagined and He opens the eyes of your heart to truth.

Decayed Foundation

As I watch this country I love meander and struggle to cling to the roots it was founded on, I pray God will direct the paths of our leaders, open the eyes of its citizens and restore this nation founded on God through His direction, peace, provision and protection. So often as I sit and read all that is going on in this country and our world, I ponder over what I can do and am overcome with a sense of helpless hope. Helplessness in the sense that there is nothing I can do, but hope in knowing God is in control and nothing happens without His hand upon the details.

This verse stung my heart as I read it today. "**When the foundations are destroyed, what can the righteous do?" Psalm 11:3**

In the chronological Bible, this Psalm comes before 2 Chronicles 7, where we find Solomon has completed the temple his father David and the Lord instructed him to build. Once completed, it says the Lord appeared to Solomon and said:

"**I have heard your prayer and have chosen this place for Myself as a temple of sacrifice. If I close the sky so there is no rain, or if I command the grasshopper to consume the land, or if I send pestilence on My people, and My people who are called by My name humble themselves, pray and seek My face, and turn from their evil ways,** then I will hear from heaven, forgive their sin, and heal their land. 2 Chronicles 7:12-14

However, if you turn away and abandon My statutes and My commands that I have set before you and if you go and serve other gods and worship them, then I will uproot Israel from the soil that I gave them, and this temple that I have sanctified for My name I will banish from My presence; I will make it an object of scorn and ridicule among all the peoples . 2 Chronicles 7:19-22

2 Chronicles 7 says that if we humble ourselves before God, seek Him and pray He will offer forgiveness and heal our land. However, if we turn away from Him, His statutes and commands (as I feel our country has done) we will be uprooted. This is God's warning to Israel and I feel we should all, as Christians and citizens of this great country, take a closer look at His warning for our own country.

While I don't have facts and figures to add, there are plenty of blogs by people much more intellectual and mathematically inclined that can offer you these details if you're curious. However, I can offer you the words and thoughts God has placed on my heart for this great nation and all of us in it. As we ponder, "What can the righteous do as the foundation is destroyed?" I pray that God will lead us deeper into His word and offer us all the wisdom, peace and direction we crave for our families and the generations to come.

Rules of Pit Dwelling

I'm always the "let's look at the bright side of things" girl. Maybe out of survival for all the things I've experienced or endured or maybe I was created with this tendency toward optimism. Honestly, it's probably a little bit of both. I've read Proverbs since I was a child, but as I approached it this time around, there was one proverb that felt as if the type had been bolded just for me.

Singing songs to a troubled heart is like taking off clothing on a cold day or like pouring vinegar on soda. Proverbs 25:20

Sometimes, people don't need an answer, or a solution or a "don't worry, be happy" song. They just need someone to cry with. Solomon wisely explains that to a weeping person, stories of unicorns and daisies can be damaging and make things worse than they already are. I know that I don't always enjoy it when someone brings sunshine to my rainy day. There are times I just need a short pity party. We certainly don't ever want to take our clothes off on a cold day or pour soda and vinegar together in our kitchen so it explodes into a grand mess we spend hours cleaning. We want to bundle up in extra clothes on a cold day and do what we can to keep the kitchen clean so we have time for what's important.

It occurs to me that Solomon's illustrations are similar to Jesus's teachings. Teachings filled with great illustrations of common things we can relate to that teach us valuable lessons.

We always hear, "Stay out or get out of the pit" since it's a dangerous place to go. Not surprisingly, I have a different angle on the pit. I'm all for the pit, *with guidelines*. I think we all reach a place now and then in life where we can benefit from getting in the pit and rolling around in our grief or misery. However, you can only go if you know you are able to get out after a few hours. You can't stay. It's like a mini-vacation, albeit a bad mini vacation, where it rains every day and the food is yucky. If you stay longer than necessary, your misery and pain can become an idol that sits higher on your priority list than God. Please know that if you suffer from depression, these words are not intended for you, as I'd encourage you to stay far way from the edge of the pit.

Rules of Pit Dwelling: You have to know you are going and ask a prayer warrior to pray for you. For example: I will say, "Ok, Kirsten I'm in the pit today. Having a little pity party for myself and rolling around in my "yuck," but I'm not planning on staying, redecorating and having cocktails. I just need to sit in this for a while, feel it and embrace it. I'm coming out tomorrow after God and I work through some things, but please pray for me and call me tomorrow and check on me to make sure I'm out."

Rejoice with those who rejoice; weep with those who weep. Romans 12:15

I don't want her to talk me out of going. I don't want her to tell me why I shouldn't go. I just want her to pray for me and love me enough to make sure I climb out after the weeping. If you have never been in the pit, I envy you. If you have, I pray you can identify when you are in it and can climb out quickly after gaining strength through the Lord. If you ever sit in that pit, I pray you know it's OK, you are only human and God is beside you. Please ask others to pray for you while you are there and hold you accountable to climb out quickly.

We can go there, but we can't stay!

Week 25

- ☐ Monday - Proverbs 27-29
- ☐ Tuesday - Ecclesiastes 1-6
- ☐ Wednesday - Ecclesiastes 7-12
- ☐ Thursday - 1 Kings 10-11; 2 Chronicles 9
- ☐ Friday - Proverbs 30-31
- ☐ Saturday - 1 Kings 12-14
- ☐ Sunday - 2 Chronicles 10-12

Week 26

- ☐ Monday - 1 Kings 15:1-24; 2 Chronicles 13-16
- ☐ Tuesday - 1 Kings 15:25-34; 1 Kings 16; 2 Chronicles 17
- ☐ Wednesday - 1 Kings 17-19
- ☐ Thursday - 1 Kings 20-21
- ☐ Friday - 1 Kings 22; 2 Chronicles 18
- ☐ Saturday - 2 Chronicles 19-23
- ☐ Sunday - Obadiah; Psalm 82-83

Revelations	
Questions	
Repeats	
Deeper Study	
Etc.	

Have You Flung God Behind Your Back?

As I have read through the Old Testament during the past several months, there is one theme that has repeated itself over and over again. God's desire for His people to obey, walk in His ways, and keep His laws and commandments is front and center in every generation. These are the words of the Lord to Solomon after he began to follow idols in the later years of his life.

"'After that, <u>if you obey</u> all I command you, <u>walk in My ways</u>, and <u>do what is right</u> in My sight in order to <u>keep My statutes and My commands</u> as My servant David did, <u>I will be with you</u>. <u>I will build you a lasting dynasty just as I built for David, and <u>I will give you Israel</u>. 1 Kings 11:38

These are the words the Lord spoke to Solomon, but throughout the OT the Lord requires this of all His people from the beginning of time. So what happens when we don't obey, walk in His ways and keep His laws? We see God's response when he speaks to Jeroboam after placing him in leadership after Solomon's son.

You behaved more wickedly than all who were before you. In order to provoke Me, you have proceeded to make for yourself other gods and cast images, but you have flung Me behind your back. 1 Kings 14:9

Wickedness, provoking God and making images to worship all make us, as the Lord said, fling Him behind our back. It always seems so obviously wrong when I'm reading it in scripture. I shake my head and wonder how His people could have turned so far from God. Then I realize that our country has turned away from God in ways that mirror His people from the OT. We allow abortion, our government officials are overcome with greed and lies, we don't allow our children to pray in school and if we stand up for Christian beliefs we are seen as narrow-minded haters. There are so many problems that can arise when we "fling God behind our backs" but one that gave me pause was this:

"This is what the LORD says: 'You have abandoned Me; therefore, I have abandoned you into the hand of Shishak" 2 Chronicles 12:5

When we abandon God, He abandons us. There isn't anything that scares me more than being abandoned by God. I have come to realize over the years how desperately I need Him for everything I do, accomplish, attempt and desire to attain (loving marriage, Godly children, a heart for Him, peace … everything!). None of it happens without God's love, courage, sustenance and guidance. I know we can't change the minds of everyone and make straight what is so crooked, but we can live out the ways and laws our God has commanded us to follow even in the face of "hardship and mockers."

High Places

Abijah rested with his fathers and was buried in the city of David. His son Asa became king in his place. During his reign the land experienced peace for 10 years. Asa did what was good and right in the sight of the LORD his God. He removed the pagan altars and the high places. He shattered their sacred pillars and chopped down their Asherah poles. He told the people of Judah to seek the LORD God of their ancestors and to carry out the instruction and the commands. He also removed the high places and the incense altars from all the cities of Judah, and the kingdom experienced peace under him. 2 Chronicles 14:1-5

Bigger and better always seems to be the way the world judges value and success. Who has the tallest buildings, biggest house, bank account or company? I love how this scripture from 2 Chronicles speaks of Asa removing the pagan alters and "high places" of Judah. Asa loved God and knew that by following His ways and laws it would lead to blessings of peace, rest and abundance.

Because the land experienced peace, Asa built fortified cities in Judah. No one made war with him in those days because the LORD gave him rest. 2 Chronicles 14:6

"High places" were the places of worship that the people of Judah had created to glorify their false gods and idols. As Asa's predecessors found out, when we take the one true God, our Creator, and demote Him from the high place in our own lives things tend to fall apart. Quickly, we see the benefits of rest, peace and blessings fall away from us. Honoring anything or anyone above the one true God has devastating effects that ripple through our lives.

I often stop and check my heart for idols. They can be so sneaky and slip in undetected! Stopping to ponder and pinpoint what has taken up residence in the high place, where only God should dwell, is vital to a strong relationship with our Father. Sometimes, either without my realizing or by own fault, I've placed finances, worry, fear, self or schedules over God. Reflecting daily on the condition of our hearts can help us serve God as Asa did and keep God in the appropriate place in our lives. For when we do, even in the midst of the biggest obstacles and trials, we can count on strength, courage and protection from the Lord. Just as Asa did when his army of 580,000 came up against an army of one million and cried out, **"LORD, there is no one besides You to help the mighty and those without strength. Help us, LORD our God, for we depend on You, and in Your name we have come against this**

large army. Yahweh, You are our God. Do not let a mere mortal hinder You" (2 Chronicles 14:11).

As we close today I ask you to prayerfully consider (along with me) these questions:

1. When you need direction, discernment, strength and courage, do you seek God or someone/something else?
2. Do you believe in your heart that there is NO ONE besides our God who should reside in the "high place" of your life?

I pray you can answer yes to these most of the days of your life, but if you can't, please know that through prayer, discipline and study God will defeat the idols that have taken over residence of your "high place." He desires to always be your guide, protector and comforter. Every single day is a battle to keep God in our high place, but He can break through the darkness with His light.

Four Little Words

Elijah is known for many things in the Bible. He was a prophet, defender of God over all other idols, and God even performed miracles for him like bringing back a boy from the dead, raining fire from the heavens. He didn't even die, but was taken up by a whirlwind instead. My point is, he was quite the man, or prophet, of God. So when I read four little words in this one verse after reading the story of God reviving the dead boy after Elijah's prayers in 1 Kings 17, I stopped dead in my tracks.

After a long time, the word of the LORD came to Elijah in the third year: "Go and present yourself to Ahab. I will send rain on the surface of the land." 1 Kings 18:1

Did you see it? He said, "After a long time."

Quickly, I wrote in the margin of my Bible, "How did Elijah feel during that time of not hearing from the Lord?" Have you ever experienced those times where God seems to have put us on hold and is taking everyone's call but ours? Or those times when you have prayed so hard for something and feel as if all your prayers are hitting a blockade before they can reach God's ears? What about the times we just can't feel His presence like we have in the past or He seems to have dropped us off in the middle of a hurricane and left us without any provisions?

I wonder if Elijah ever felt like that? Here we have a man of God, a prophet, whom God has been so close to, revealed weather patterns to him and listened so closely to his prayers He raised a boy from the dead, and then … silence for "a long time." God went silent on Elijah. I wonder if he felt like I have when those desert times have hit. Did he feel vulnerable and lonely? Did he wonder if he had done something wrong or had some sin in his heart he hadn't confessed? Did he think his purpose for God's kingdom had been fulfilled and God had moved on to the next person to do the prophesying?

I know that when I go through time like Elijah experienced, a short time can feel like an eternity, but it's always a great reminder of how much I rely on God in my life and how much His presence and gentle whisper mean to me and guide me. I can't say I'm always ready to respond to Him with wild abandon, but I yearn to serve Him and seek His ways. When I can't sense Him, it stirs my soul, and I begin to seek Him more and more. **As a deer longs for streams of water, so I long for You, God. (Psalm 2:1)** He is always close, but maybe that's why He quiets Himself from time to time. To stir our hearts, create appreciation, desire and open our eyes to how much we truly need Him in our daily lives.

Got Angry?

After studying the book of Zechariah and being completely blessed and blown away by this amazing book of the Bible I had never considered reading, it made me wonder how many other small and less popular books of the Bible might be hiding something equally awe–inspiring.

After all, every bit of the Bible is God's word, not just the most popular books like Genesis, the Gospels, Acts, Psalms, James, etc. So I decided to look into the book of Obadiah. I found that it's about how we feel after being taken advantage of, when we are wronged or betrayed by someone we trust. Obadiah reminds us that it's God's job to handle our enemies, not ours.

It's written by Obadiah himself who was an unknown prophet with a powerful message. He reminds us that we can count on God's loyalty, and trust Him to handle those who rob us, bring disaster to our lives, pillage our joy, deceive us, overpower us and set traps for us (Obadiah 1:5-7).

You should not gloat over your brother in the day of his misfortune, nor rejoice over the people of Judah in the day of their destruction, nor boast so much in the day of their trouble. You should not march through the gates of my people in the day of their disaster, nor gloat over them in their calamity in the day of their disaster, nor seize their wealth in the day of their disaster. You should not wait at the

91

crossroads to cut down their fugitives, nor hand over their survivors in the day of their trouble. Obadiah 1:12-14

In verses 12-14 it says we should never "rejoice over their destruction, boast over their troubles, or look down on" the people who treat us terribly. That's a tough one to swallow, but God promises that all they have done to you will return upon their own heads (v. 15). You can count on God's loyalty, you can trust Him to handle those who have brought you sorrow, disaster, shame and hurt (Obadiah 1:5-7).

Other than the obvious lesson of letting God handle your battles, your revenge and your enemies that we learned in Obadiah, I'd like to also point out that:

1. Even though Obadiah was an unknown prophet, only has one chapter in his book and you don't hear his words mentioned much in sermons, His message is from the Lord. It's important we *study the entire Bible* so we don't miss a word from the Lord.

2. It's also important to understand that no matter how insignificant your story or faith my seem to you, with God it has the power to touch others in ways you could never imagine. You have an awesome story that He wants you to *share with others for His glory*.

 Notes and Reflections:

Week 27

- ☐ Monday - 2 Kings 1-4
- ☐ Tuesday - 2 Kings 5-8
- ☐ Wednesday - 2 Kings 9-11
- ☐ Thursday - 2 Kings 12-13; 2 Chronicles 24
- ☐ Friday - 2 Kings 14; 2 Chronicles 25
- ☐ Saturday - Jonah 1-4
- ☐ Sunday - 2 Kings 15; 2 Chronicles 26

Week 28

- ☐ Monday - Isaiah 1-4
- ☐ Tuesday - Isaiah 5-8
- ☐ Wednesday - Amos 1-5
- ☐ Thursday - Amos 6-9
- ☐ Friday - 2 Chronicles 27; Isaiah 9-12
- ☐ Saturday - Micah 1-7
- ☐ Sunday - 2 Chronicles 28; 2 Kings 16-17

Revelations	
Questions	
Repeats	
Deeper Study	
Etc.	

Wholeheartedly

Throughout the books of 2 Chronicles and 2 Kings we find chapter after chapter of the legacies of the Kings of Judah and Israel. It's quite tedious to read and a bit confusing at times with all the names, wars and family trees, but we do find a common theme running through all of their stories. They either "did what was right in the sight of the Lord" and were blessed and provided protection or "they did what was evil in the Lord's sight" and found themselves subject to conspiracy, war and turmoil. And then came Amaziah.

Amaziah became king when he was 25 years old and reigned 29 years in Jerusalem. His mother's name was Jehoaddan; she was from Jerusalem. He did what was right in the LORD's sight but not wholeheartedly. 2 Chronicles 25:1-2

We are told that Amaziah did what was right, but not "wholeheartedly." This word caught my eye and I was convicted in my heart as I read it. The definition of wholeheartedly is, "marked by unconditional commitment, unstinting devotion, or unreserved enthusiasm" (thefreedictionary.com). We find that Amaziah followed the ways of the Lord when he executed the two servants who had murdered his father (v.3), but did not have their children put to death because—as it is written in the Law, in the book of Moses, the LORD commands— **"Fathers must not die because of children, and children must not die because of fathers, but each one will die for his own sin." (v.4)**

However, when faced with an intimidating battle he quickly brought in the **"gods of the Seirites and set them up as his gods. He worshiped them and burned incense to them" (v.14).** He knew the ways and laws of the Lord and had obviously tried to live by them and honor them at one point, but when the going got tough he turned to idols. He wasn't serving with his whole heart!

95

So the LORD's anger was against Amaziah, and He sent a prophet to him, who said, **"Why have you sought a people's gods that could not deliver their own people from your hand?" (v.15).** Why did Amaziah turn from the Lord? I wonder if his faith started to falter when faced with death or the fear of losing his power. Did he feel like God wasn't enough and thought he needed some back-up? Was he overcome with peer pressure from the idol worshippers that surrounded him? He was on the right track at some point and I wonder what happened or how his heart changed to make him stumble and not serve the Lord wholeheartedly.

Amaziah's story resonates with me. I think of how often I have let pride, the illusion of control and a lack of faithfulness cause me to stumble and not serve God with my whole heart. Sure, I have good intentions, but then I let the doubt, fear, anger, resentment, pride or other idol have its way with me and my whole heart turns to just three-quarters or a half. I consider the anger that God had for Amaziah and how once he turned his back on the Lord and stopped following Him, **"a conspiracy was formed against him in Jerusalem, and he fled to Lachish. However, men were sent after him to Lachish, and they put him to death there. (v. 27)**

We will falter, fail and flee sometimes, but our God is always calling us back to Him. We don't have to keep running. We need only turn our hearts back and place our eyes on Him to return under His wing of love, forgiveness and protection. Being a Christian doesn't make us perfect, but it does make us forgiven and reconciled back to Christ. If you have turned from the ways of the Lord, as Amaziah did, it isn't too late to turn back and serve God wholeheartedly once again. His greatest gift and desire for us is the redemption He alone can offer through the blood of His son Jesus. Will you accept that gift today?

Appointed

Ah, the book of Jonah. What a refreshing story to read with eyes that have been deep into Chronicles and Kings for weeks of history, wars and the legacies of kings. My first instinct was to just skim this story because I've read the book and sung the songs of Jonah's journey about a zillion times. What more could I really get out of this story? As God would have it, and always does, something new. That's the beauty of Bible's story, it never stops teaching, guiding, rebuking and showing us ways to live closer to our Heavenly Father.

So far, through the Old Testament, we have seen God appoint angels to deliver visions, prophets to deliver messages and kings to lead countries. However, as I read Jonah with fresh eyes this year, I noticed the word "appointed" repeated over and over, but God wasn't appointing "people" this time. In the book of Jonah we see God appoint the creatures and elements of His creation to lead and guide Jonah to Nineveh and teach him lessons of love. Let's take a look.

After Jonah receives the word of the Lord to head to Nineveh and deliver His message of "you better straighten up or you will be destroyed," Jonah hits the road to hide from the Lord, but who can hide from the Lord? **"Now the LORD had appointed a huge fish to swallow Jonah, and Jonah was in the fish three days and three nights." (Jonah 1:17)**

God appoints a huge fish. I love it! Anyone who claims we don't serve a creative God hasn't read this story. So, after Jonah and God have some alone time, in the belly of the huge fish, he gets vomited out to complete his task. I wonder if Jonah is regretting taking the hard way at this point in the story? I have been there. Trying to go my own way and ignore the path God has set before me never gets me to far and usually just adds some additional heartache and delays the inevitable.

But God wasn't done appointing … in chapter 4 He appoints a plant, a worm and a scorching east wind to open the eyes of a pouting Jonah who was disappointed God forgave the people of Nineveh and relented from His plans of destroying them after they repented. These verses remind that our God is the Creator of all we see and don't see. He is in every detail of everything that has happened, is happening and will happen. He is the same today as he was and always will be. Our hearts may waver, but His remains steady. His hand is on all of creation and His plan is perfect. I pray we will begin to see God at work in all that is around us each day. Our God cares for us more than we can ever imagine. So much so, He is in the movement of the tiniest creatures and can still hear each prayer you pray and count each tear that falls from your face.

Reflect on Jonah 4:6-11 before moving on.

Send ME!

Recently, my husband and I had the privilege of being at home a few nights alone while our children were visiting their grandparents. On our second evening together, we sat in the window of a new Raleigh restaurant we decided to try at the last minute. It was quiet and lovely with a view of the street. We had just finished eating our dinner when I looked up and noticed an elderly woman who was trying to traverse the gravel drive and cross the street with a package in one hand and a cane in another. She was shaky and I knew if she fell she would never make the dinner party she was surly trying to attend. As I watched, I heard God whisper, "Who should I send?" I quickly and apologetically looked at my husband and said, "I've got to go. I'm going to help that woman cross and street and get into the restaurant. I'll be back." As I approached I explained my desire to help her make it to her destination. She graciously allowed me to carry her package and took my arm as we slowly made our way to another restaurant nearby.

As it turned out, she had made a very special effort to attend a dear friend's birthday dinner. I got her all the way to her seat, wished her friend a happy birthday and rushed back to my husband. It's not always convenient to answer God's call, it can even be a little intimidating and awkward (like the day I prayed with a woman who was getting her first mammogram in the middle of the waiting room while we were clothed in our matching pink tops), but it is always such a blessing and feels amazing to know that God can use this sinful and unworthy servant to do His great works.

Then I heard the voice of the LORD saying: Who should I send? Who will go for Us? I said: Here I am. Send me. Isaiah 6:8

Unlike Moses and Jeremiah, Isaiah was ready to roll when God called upon him to share His message with Israel. I love how Isaiah never questioned God or his own capabilities. He probably knew that his message would not result in leading God's people to repentance to avoid destruction and catastrophe, but he went anyway. He shared, he prophesied, he tried! Most of all, he answered God's call. "Who should I send? Who will go for us?" said the Lord. I pray we all stand up tall and answer, "Send me, God! Send me!"

Fall Away

Reading the book of Isaiah has had a great impact on me. Over and over again, it reminds us not just how far God's people fell from His ways and laws, but how big and powerful God's anger can grow when we continually turn away from Him after receiving warning after warning and second chance after second chance. It's not a side of God I think about as often as I probably should. Isaiah was a prophet sent to warn the people to repent so they could avoid calamity, but the residents of Jerusalem would not listen. Isaiah 5:20-24 says this of the people:

Woe to those who call evil good and good evil, who substitute darkness for light and light for darkness, who substitute bitter for sweet and sweet for bitter. Woe to those who are wise in their own opinion and clever in their own sight. Woe to those who are heroes at drinking wine, who are fearless at mixing beer, who acquit the guilty for a bribe and deprive the innocent of justice ... for they have rejected the instruction of the LORD of Hosts, and they have despised the word of the Holy One of Israel.

It's not this that strikes fear in my heart, it's how much the residents of Jerusalem remind me of our country presently and how much the Lord's anger burns against those who have rejected His instruction and despised His words. I won't go into every detail here, but what Isaiah shares with the inhabitants of the land about what will come if there is no repentance isn't pretty: mountains quake, corpses are like bodies in the street, cities lie in ruin, the land is desolate, etc. (Isaiah 25-30 is a small picture of this). Honestly, even though this is about God's people from long ago, it has brought up some dialogue in my mind with God about redemption and the direction our nation and the world are taking. Where do my family and I fit into all of this as we try to live lives worthy of the gospel? All that said, here are the words God revealed to Isaiah:

For this is what the LORD said to me with great power, to keep me from going the way of this people: Do not call everything an alliance

these people say is an alliance. Do not fear what they fear; do not be terrified. You are to regard only the LORD of Hosts as holy. Only He should be feared; only He should be held in awe. Isaiah 8:11-13

I wonder if Isaiah felt as I have when he received the news of the impending destruction? Did fear begin to creep into his soul? Was he wondering where he fit into this story and why bother trying to save people who didn't want to be saved? I'm so thankful for God's words in Isaiah 8. They are a reminder to me, and all of us, that as Christ followers there is only one we should follow and fear – Our Lord and Savior – all else should fall away. The ending of our story has already been written. The Lord has won! He has conquered, so we need not fear what others fear. Amen!

Reminders from Amos

Amos was an average shepherd who became one of the first prophets from 8th century B.C. I've read from the book of Amos here and there, but never studied it closely until now. It's quite beautiful and a bit scary too. His book and speaking was one of warning, as he foretold of God's judgement. However, being on this side of history, we have seen those judgements fulfilled. That said, it is a great reminder and brings on many strong feelings in my heart concerning the day the Lord returns to claim this place and His people.

In my opinion, one of the best things about reading scripture is that we discover God's character. When we know Him, we can recognize Him around us and at work in our lives. People ask me all the time how I see God in my daily life. All I can say is that, to see someone and recognize them, you must know them first. Humbling me day after day for years, God has shown me how discipline and obedience is critical to following

Him wholeheartedly. Getting to know Him, His ways and His truths through scripture is half of the formula and prayer is the other. Amos shared some amazing passages that remind us who the God we serve really is. Take a look at the first two:

He is here: the One who forms the mountains, creates the wind, and reveals His thoughts to man, the One who makes the dawn out of darkness and strides on the heights of the earth. Yahweh, the God of Hosts, is His name. Amos 4:13

The One who made the Pleiades and Orion, who turns darkness into dawn and darkens day into night, who summons the waters of the sea and pours them out over the face of the earth—Yahweh is His name. Amos 5:8

It's exhilarating and scary (in a good way). Exhilarating because I can say this God is a friend of mine who adores me and died for me. Scary, because as I look at my life there are many days I forget the splendor and magnitude of the One I serve. I need these verses printed out and framed all over my house as a reminder of His sovereignty and mighty ways every moment of my days. Especially on the days my wits are frazzled and my heart is breaking over fear, sadness or trial. What better way to trust and live than to remember our God is so much greater than all we see, think and fear? As you read this last verse I pray you will sit for a minute or two and allow the depth and enormity of our God soak into your reality.

He builds His upper chambers in the heavens and lays the foundation of His vault on the earth. He summons the waters of the sea and pours them out on the face of the earth. Yahweh is His name. Amos 9:6

Week 29

- ☐ Monday - Isaiah 13-17
- ☐ Tuesday - Isaiah 18-22
- ☐ Wednesday - Isaiah 23-27
- ☐ Thursday - 2 Kings 18:1-8; 2 Chronicles 29-31; Psalm 48
- ☐ Friday - Hosea 1-7
- ☐ Saturday - Hosea 8-14
- ☐ Sunday - Isaiah 28-30

Week 30

- ☐ Monday - Isaiah 31-34
- ☐ Tuesday - Isaiah 35-36
- ☐ Wednesday - Isaiah 37-39; Psalm 76
- ☐ Thursday - Isaiah 40-43
- ☐ Friday - Isaiah 44-48
- ☐ Saturday - 2 Kings 18:9-37; 2 Kings 19; Psalm 46, 80, 135
- ☐ Sunday - Isaiah 49-53

Revelations	
Questions	
Repeats	
Deeper Study	
Etc.	

Famine of Words

Hear this! The days are coming— this is the declaration of the LORD God— when I will send a famine through the land: not a famine of bread or a thirst for water, but of hearing the words of the LORD. Amos 8:11

The definition of famine is any extreme and general scarcity; extreme hunger for; starvation.

When Amos and Hosea speak of Israel's corruption and God's disgust, I can't help but imagine He feels the same about our country at this time. In so many ways we have turned our backs on Him, His ways and laws just as the Israelites had. Amos 8:11 describes God sending a famine "of hearing from the Lord" and it stung my heart in a way that I had not anticipated. One of my greatest prayers is that God will continue to create a thirst for Him in my heart that can't be quenched. Not hearing from Him is one of my greatest fears. How would I parent my children, keep my marriage together, live a life worthy of the Gospel, be His light in the world or trust in my forgiveness of sin if I couldn't hear from Him? My communication with God is a connection I pray will never be broken.

Consider all that the Lord had done for His people throughout the Old Testament so far, only to have them turn their backs on Him. I know how I feel when I've served, entertained and loved on my children all day only for it to end in tears over one small thing that didn't go their way. It's as if all the other actions of love never existed. I'm hurt and I feel disrespected, unappreciated and incredibly frustrated.

Woe to them, for they fled from Me; destruction to them, for they rebelled against Me! Though I want to redeem them, they speak lies

105

against Me. I trained and strengthened their arms, but they plot evil against Me. . . They turn, but not to what is above; they are like a faulty bow. Hosea 7:13, 15-16

God gives, gives and gives. He forgives, forgives and forgives. He relents, relents and relents some more, but how long can He allow that to occur if we won't wake up, open our eyes and turn back to Him, seek Him and search for Him? That's why we need those times of silence and famine. At some point, a parent has to leave a child to their own devices until they reach rock bottom and there is no other place to look but up. Hopefully then, sin is recognized and our search for God and a desire for His presence will overcome once again.

I will depart and return to My place until they recognize their guilt and seek My face; they will search for Me in their distress. Hosea 5:15

The Only Help

Woe to those who go down to Egypt for help and who depend on horses! They trust in the abundance of chariots and in the large number of horsemen. They do not look to the Holy One of Israel and they do not seek the LORD's help. Isaiah 31:1

I realize these passages describe the fact that God's people were relying more on other countries and their resources for protection than they were God, but it made me realize once again how often we are just like Israel in our personal lives. Couldn't this verse also read: Woe to those who turn to shopping, busyness and depend only on themselves. They trust in self and the abundance of material things. Instead of looking to God for provision and protection they build up earthly treasures instead

106

of Heavenly ones. Woe to those who have forgotten to honor the ways and laws of the Lord and have allowed their hearts to be swayed by earthly desires.

That makes it a little more personal doesn't it? How often do we skip the most important step when faced with daily decisions big and small? How often do we allow pride to overtake our hearts, so we fail to seek God's desires above our own selfish desires? Yikes, right?! If you had my Bible in your hand, it would amaze you to see how many times the word "Yikes!" is written in the margin. Its passages of scripture are a powerful and bold reminder that we must turn from other idols and only serve God. Repentance is non-negotiable! It's a must! The Lord alone is the only one who can save us, redeem us and complete us.

Woe to those of us who forget to seek the face of God daily, but thankfully we have Jesus! So we can have faith that when we forget ... there is the blood of Christ that was shed for us so that we can have forgiveness and be reconciled back to Him with a simple, but humble, request.

LORD, be gracious to us! We wait for You.
Be our strength every morning
and our salvation in time of trouble. Isaiah 33:2

 Notes and Reflections:

Week 31

- ☐ Monday - Isaiah 54-58
- ☐ Tuesday - Isaiah 59-63
- ☐ Wednesday - Isaiah 64-66
- ☐ Thursday - 2 Kings 20-21
- ☐ Friday - 2 Chronicles 32-33
- ☐ Saturday - Nahum 1-3
- ☐ Sunday - 2 Kings 22-23; 2 Chronicles 34-35

Week 32

- ☐ Monday - Zephaniah 1-3
- ☐ Tuesday - Jeremiah 1-3
- ☐ Wednesday - Jeremiah 4-6
- ☐ Thursday - Jeremiah 7-9
- ☐ Friday - Jeremiah 10-13
- ☐ Saturday - Jeremiah 14-17
- ☐ Sunday - Jeremiah 18-22

Revelations	
Questions	
Repeats	
Deeper Study	
Etc.	

Three Pauses

In 2 Kings 20 we read about Hezekiah becoming terminally ill and praying to God to be healed.

"Please LORD, remember how I have walked before You faithfully and wholeheartedly and have done what pleases You." And Hezekiah wept bitterly. 2 Kings 20:3

God hears, answers his prayer and send a message through the prophet Isaiah. **"Go back and tell Hezekiah, the leader of My people, 'This is what the LORD God of your ancestor David says: I have heard your prayer; I have seen your tears. Look, I will heal you. On the third day from now you will go up to the LORD's temple. I will add 15 years to your life. I will deliver you and this city from the hand of the king of Assyria. I will defend this city for My sake and for the sake of My servant David.'" 2 Kings 20:5-6**

This is such a beautiful image. God saying, "I have heard your prayers and seen your tears" brings up swells of thanksgiving and praise in my heart. We don't always receive the answers we request in our prayers like Hezekiah did this time, but God always hears our prayers and sees our tears. We might be tempted to stop here at the miracle of God granting him 15 more years of life, but let's keep going.

While Hezekiah was sick, the son of the king of Babylon (Merodach-baladan) sent him letters and a gift wishing him well. Hezekiah thought this was a very kind gesture and invited Merodach-baladan to visit his house and showed him every treasure in it. In fact, there was nothing in his palace and in all his realm that Hezekiah did not show them (v. 13).

This was my first pause. Why would Hezekiah do such a thing? When

110

someone sends me a birthday gift or soup when I'm sick, I usually just write them a thank you note. I don't invite them over to my house and show them all my jewelry, plates, lamps and grandma's china. I wonder if Hezekiah was feeling prideful (instead of thankful) that the Lord had saved him and just wanted to show off all he had in his kingdom. I'm not sure, but the story becomes more interesting. Isaiah hears from the Lord once again and delivers the word of the Lord to Hezekiah after hearing about his show and tell.

'The time will certainly come when everything in your palace and all that your fathers have stored up until this day will be carried off to Babylon; nothing will be left,' says the LORD. 'Some of your descendants who come from you will be taken away, and they will become eunuchs in the palace of the king of Babylon'" (v. 17-18)

Wow, Hezekiah's pride session just gave away the locations of the kingdom's treasures. This is important because on the day the Babylonians would overtake his land, they would be able to march in and know exactly where to find it all. Then, Hezekiahs' response gave me *my second pause.*

Then Hezekiah said to Isaiah, "The word of the LORD that you have spoken is good," for he thought: Why not, if there will be peace and security during my lifetime? (v. 19)

What? Hezekiah gets a heads up on what will happen for future generations and says, "OK, that's cool." All while thinking "at least everything will be OK while I'm around." My selfish alert just went off again. I think of my Dad who mourns for the way this country is currently headed with terrorism and corroded morals. He mourns not for himself (he is 87), but for me and my children who will have to live in the midst of all this mess and turmoil. Notice how Hezekiah said one

111

thing and thought another. I think if Hezekiah said "what you have spoken is good" because he thought he deserved it after his prideful show and tell, he would have thought, "I really messed this up for future generations of my people. I need to keep my pride more in check." Instead, he thought "Oh well, at least things will be peaceful in my lifetime."

The definition of pride is a feeling or deep pleasure or satisfaction derived from one's own achievements, the achievements of those with whom one is closely associated, or from qualities or possessions that are widely admired.

My third and final pause is this: How does my pride effect those around me in the short-term and the long? My children, husband, friends, family and all I come in contact with? How often has pride kept me from doing the right thing in God's sight? Kept me from being a light in this dark world?

God, please shine a light on my pride so that every time it starts to sneak into my heart I recognize it quickly, pray for you to overcome it and remember that it is only by your power, your might and your strength that I can stand tall and be a light in this dark world. All I have, need and desire should be from you and you alone. I'm so grateful that it's not up to me alone, that you walk each step with me, hear me and are always found in times of trouble. Amen.

Favorably

Sifting through Isaiah this week I uncovered a little nugget of truth hidden in Isaiah 66:2.

My hand made all these things,
and so they all came into being.
This is the LORD's declaration.
I will look favorably on this kind of person:
one who is humble, submissive in spirit,
and trembles at My word.

In this one verse, the Lord declares that He will look favorably upon a person with three qualities. Let's sit on this verse today and consider what is required in order to be this kind of person. First, the Lord desires someone who is humble.

The definition of humble is someone who is not proud; not thinking of yourself as better than other people; given or said in a way that shows you do not think you are better than other people; showing that you do not think of yourself as better than other people.

Second, the Lord is looking for a submissive spirit. This word has such a negative association in our world today. Look closely at the definition. The definition of submissive is willing to obey someone else.

Submitting to someone doesn't mean rolling over and playing dead; it's just a willingness to obey someone other than yourself. God desires for us to seek His wisdom and ways and be willing obey Him, even when it's uncomfortable or doesn't seem to make sense. To look past our own selfish desires and motives to be a part of a BIGGER story. His story.

Thirdly, God is looking for those who tremble at His Word. So often, we associate trembling with fear, but the definition of tremble is to shake slightly because you are afraid, nervous, excited, etc.; to shake slightly because of some force.

113

God wants to see us reacting in awe, excitement, fear and anticipation to His written word. Maybe our bodies will even react in actual movement with a shiver or a shudder. If I had a penny for every time I've gotten goose bumps as I read God's word we could all sit down and enjoy some frozen yogurt while we discussed these three qualities.

This world is a mess, but our God is still in control. He is not surprised by anything that has happened or will happen. However, through it all, He is looking for those who are humble, submissive, and tremble at His word. Take a few moments today to sit in meditation and prayer with God about these three qualities. Ask Him to reveal where you have flaws and to give you His strength and courage to make the changes that are required for you to be one of those He looks upon favorably.

Lost It?

Keep the charge of the LORD your God, walking in his ways and keeping his statutes, his commandments, his rules, and his testimonies, as it is written in the Law of Moses, that you may prosper in all that you do and wherever you turn. 1 Kings 2:3

As I read about King Josiah this week, I was reminded about an old post from October 2012 I had written on the lost book of law. I dug it out for you today.

"You didn't tell me not to do it today" my son argued. "Son, I didn't think I had to tell you the same rule every day. When I tell you once, that stands for everyday!" I reinforced with a not so happy tone in my voice. Repeating the same thing over and over again is part of a mom's life. It can be so frustrating to ask my kids not to do something one day, only to have them "forget" the next day. Does it all fall out every night when they are sleeping?

This all came to mind as I was revisiting the story of King Josiah. My son is 10, but Josiah was only 8 years old when he became king. Can you imagine? I'm sure he had many servants to pick up after him. Josiah reigned Jerusalem for 31 years. Who says the Bible doesn't have some good stories?!

And Hilkiah the high priest said to Shaphan the secretary, "I have found the Book of the Law in the house of the LORD." And Hilkiah gave the book to Shaphan, and he read it. 2 Kings 22:8

Here's the crazy thing that stood out to me as I revisited this story. Notice what 2 Kings 22:8 (above) says. "I found the Book of Law." The Book of Law, which was God's directions and laws for his people, had been either hidden or misplaced for years and years. They didn't even know what the book was until they began to read it, because it had been forgotten by previous generations. This is difficult to comprehend when we live in a world where I alone probably have 20 different types of Bibles in my house, but it's true. They had lost it and were living the laws that had been watered down after years mixed in with whatever else had come along.

When the king heard the words of the Book of the Law, he tore his clothes. And the king commanded Hilkiah the priest, and Ahikam the son of Shaphan, and Achbor the son of Micaiah, and Shaphan the secretary, and Asaiah the king's servant, saying, "Go, inquire of the LORD for me, and for the people, and for all Judah, concerning the words of this book that has been found. For great is the wrath of the LORD that is kindled against us, because our fathers have not obeyed

the words of this book, to do according to all that is written concerning us." 2 Kings 22:11-13

So when The Book of Law was found and King Josiah heard the words read from it he "tore his clothes." Can you imagine discovering something that gave you every key and insight into how you needed to live for God and recognizing you had been doing the opposite in most cases? Josiah tore at his clothes because he was beside himself with despair, anguish and regret. They had been getting it all wrong, but God honored Josiah because he quickly repented, turned from idols and went back to observing festivals and following God's laws.

So Josiah removed everything that was detestable from all the lands belonging to the Israelites, and he required all who were present in Israel to serve the LORD their God. Throughout his reign they did not turn aside from following Yahweh, the God of their ancestors. 2 Chronicles 34:33

We go through times like this in our own lives. We live like God's word has been lost. We live as if we don't remember His ways, His truths and His commandments. Then, by the grace of God, we find it again and hopefully mourn our sin and begin to live according to His ways once more. You may have lost it for a while, but God has never given up on you. You may have lost it for a while, but God still loves you. You may have lost it for a while, but God can still turn your failures into His triumphs. Return to Him today. We may let go of Him, but He never lets go of us! With God there is always hope.

The Dirge Report

No, that isn't a typo (I didn't mean to type the Drudge Report©). One of the most exciting parts of reading the Bible is making new discoveries every time you open it up. Most recently, I discovered a new word. Well, new to me. **Dirge** is a slow song that expresses deep sadness or sorrow. Honestly, I have no recollection of ever having read or heard this word until reading it in 2 Chronicles.

As this point in 2 Chronicles, we find King Josiah being a bit stubborn and heading off to the Valley of Megiddo to fight the King of Egypt (Neco). We even read that Neco tells him not to come and that these are God's words. Not surprisingly, this leads to a mortal wound by Neco's archers which then results in a mourning kingdom. King Josiah had been the one who led the Israelites back to God after finding and then following God's laws and decrees. He rebuilt the temple and began celebrating the appointed festivals. He was the last incredible leader the Israelites had before its destruction. He had basically led Israel through a revival, and now he was gone.

Read 2 Chronicles 35:20-25.

The entire kingdom was deeply saddened and mourned his death. This is where our new word comes in. Jeremiah chants a dirge (song of sorrow) over Josiah. It's his funeral song, his ceremony, his wake. Commentators say that his obituary was full of all the positive things Josiah had done for the Israelites by honoring and turning back to God. All that said, the overarching thought that has stayed with me (besides a new vocabulary word) is this: What will they sing over me? Who will sing my dirge and will it be positive? Will they be able to say that I laid down my life and lived for the Lord? That I gave in a sacrificial way?

Gave my children a strong foundation to guide them? Honored my husband and humbled myself before others? This Christmas season, I pray God will guide each of us with a willing heart to do all these things and more for Him in the time He has given us.

Word Watching

I found something so exciting in Jeremiah. Let's set the stage: The Lord calls upon Jeremiah to go and speak without fear about all He shares with him. Jeremiah, like many before him, says, **"Oh no, LORD, GOD! Look, I don't know how to speak since I am only a youth" (Jeremiah 1:6).** And then the LORD reaches out His hand to touch Jeremiah's mouth and tells him, **"I have now filled your mouth with My words." (v. 9)**

This makes my heart leap. Have you ever been in one of those situations where you have been able to speak a gentle truth, offer a loving comfort or submissively follow in a way that you know you otherwise would have never been able to do if God hadn't stretched out His hand and filled your mouth with His words and your heart with His love? What a powerful moment. I'm so thankful God doesn't allow me to get in the way of His plan and uses me to do something I never thought capable for His glory. Of course, we are always capable when we say, "Not me, but You God!"

Jeremiah's story doesn't end there, as God goes on to give Jeremiah two visions. Today we'll explore the first together, and then I hope you will dig into the book of Jeremiah to read about the second vision.

Then the word of the LORD came to me, asking, "What do you see, Jeremiah?" I replied, "I see a branch of an almond tree." The LORD said to me, "You have seen correctly, for I watch over My word to accomplish it." Again the word of the LORD came to me inquiring, "What do you see?" Jeremiah 1:11-13

When I read the words "… for I watch over My word to accomplish it" it was as though they leapt off the page. This is the kind of revelation and reminder that keeps me coming back day after day to God's word. We often envision God looking down on us and watching over us, but have you ever considered that He watches over His word so that it is accomplished?! Those nine words make my arms raise in joy, my eyes look to the heavens, my heart leap with gladness and my spirit soar with faith and hope. I know and trust God's word to be from Him. I believe every word penned by human hands He guided and allowed to enter His holy text, but to picture Him watching over His word is such an incredible image and a great reminder. God is close! He is in every teeny tiny detail, He see all, knows all and will accomplish all He has promised and declared.

What an awesome God we serve. I pray we honor Him in all our ways, praise Him for His power, embrace Him with all our hearts and serve Him with every cell. He is here, He is always near and He is in control so we can set all fear and uncertainty aside.

Dirty Underwear

Again, God has blown my mind, surprised me and made me smile. How have I missed this little nugget in Jeremiah in my years of reading the Bible? I love how God continues to teach His people and prophets through everyday ordinary things. Take a look at what the Lord shows Jeremiah through dirty underwear. Yes, underwear.

This is what the LORD said to me: "Go and buy yourself a linen undergarment and put it on, but do not put it in water." So I bought underwear as the LORD instructed me and put it on. Then the word of the LORD came to me a second time: "Take the underwear that you bought and are wearing, and go at once to the Euphrates and hide it in a rocky crevice." So I went and hid it by the Euphrates, as the LORD commanded me. Jeremiah 13:1-5

The Lord has placed a lot of things on my heart over the years, but He has never urged me to purchase underwear, wear it for a while and then hide in under a rock by the creek in our backyard for a while. Let's not miss how obedient Jeremiah is when the Lord speaks to Him. This is an unusual request, but Jeremiah never questioned why or what in the world for, He just followed the Lord's command. Then Jeremiah tells us (v. 6-7) that "a long time later" the Lord tells him to return to the same spot where he hid the underwear and dig it up. OK, maybe even a little stranger until you keep reading. Of course, Jeremiah finds what you would expect: old, dirty, stinky and maybe even decaying underwear that are of no use. Where is God going with all of this?

Then the word of the LORD came to me: "This is what the LORD says: Just like this I will ruin the great pride of both Judah and Jerusalem. These evil people, who refuse to listen to Me, who follow the stubbornness of their own hearts, and who have followed other gods to serve and worship—they will be like this underwear, of no use at all. Just as underwear clings to one's waist, so I fastened the whole house of Israel and of Judah to Me"—this is the LORD's declaration— "so that they might be My people for My fame, praise, and glory, but they would not obey. Jeremiah 13:8-11

120

In these verses, God uses the dirty underwear to illustrate how useless the people who have turned from His ways are to Him and foretells of their ruin. For us, this is a wonderful reminder to look for God in the ordinary. Using tangible illustrations that I will understand and be able to comprehend is one of the great ways He teaches me His ways and truth every day of my life. Not only that, it reminds us that when we put God aside and refuse to listen to Him we are nothing more than dirty underwear and useless for His kingdom. I don't know about you, but I want to be like the elastic waist in that underwear that "clings" to my Heavenly Father. Who knew underwear could teach us so much? I love our God!

 Notes and Reflections:

Week 33

- ☐ Monday - Jeremiah 23-25
- ☐ Tuesday - Jeremiah 26-29
- ☐ Wednesday - Jeremiah 30-31
- ☐ Thursday - Jeremiah 32-34
- ☐ Friday - Jeremiah 35-37
- ☐ Saturday - Jeremiah 38-40; Psalm 74, 79
- ☐ Sunday - 2 Kings 24-25; 2 Chronicles 36

Week 34

- ☐ Monday - Habakkuk 1-3
- ☐ Tuesday - Jeremiah 41-45
- ☐ Wednesday - Jeremiah 46-48
- ☐ Thursday - Jeremiah 49-50
- ☐ Friday - Jeremiah 51-52
- ☐ Saturday - Lamentations 1; Lamentations 2; Lamentations 3:1-36
- ☐ Sunday - Lamentations 3:37-66; Lamentations 4 & 5

Revelations	
Questions	
Repeats	
Deeper Study	
Etc.	

Under the Hood

"For I know the plans I have for you"—this is the LORD's declaration—"plans for your welfare, not for disaster, to give you a future and a hope." Jeremiah 29:11

Running across this verse in Jeremiah made me stop and think for a moment. We have all heard, seen and probably have this verse in our homes somewhere. They are wonderful words to remember and reflect on in our daily lives. Remembering God has our backs, has a Master plan for each of us and has us in the palm of His hand is something I certainly need at the forefront of my mind. However, I think too often we look to verses for our own purposes and forget to consider the context they are found in. We miss the deeper meaning and magnitude of the words spoken when we do this.

Jeremiah 29:11 is only one verse (out of 25) taken from, **"the text of the letter that Jeremiah the prophet sent from Jerusalem to the rest of the elders of the exiles, the priests, the prophets, and all the people Nebuchadnezzar had deported from Jerusalem to Babylon" (Jeremiah 29:1).**

God's people, who had their city plundered and people taken prisoner to Babylon, certainly needed to hear there were brighter days ahead. That God had not forgotten them completely, despite their evil ways. This was the news they had waited for. God's promise that after 70 years He would restore them and as verse 14 says, **restore their fortunes, gather them up from where He has driven them and bring them back to the place from which He sent them to exile.**

Can you imagine how much this promise meant to God's people, especially as they were being held captive as prisoners? When we explore beyond the surface meaning of God's word, we discover deeper meanings behind His story and promises.

How about this one from Jeremiah?

Call to Me and I will answer you and tell you great and incomprehensible things you do not know. Jeremiah 33:3

This is a wonderful reminder for us that all we need to do is ask God for help, wisdom, grace, forgiveness, patience ... the list goes on and on. Ask and we will find, right? But, consider that these words came to Jeremiah as he was still confined in the guard's courtyard, still in trouble, still feeling isolated for prophesying the Lord's words. The Lord arrives right on time and tells him about the restoration of Israel.

While he was still confined in the guard's courtyard, the word of the LORD came to Jeremiah a second time: "The LORD who made the earth, the LORD who forms it to establish it, Yahweh is His name, says this: Call to Me and I will answer you and tell you great and incomprehensible things you do not know. Jeremiah 33:1-3

Context and meaning are vital to understand and give life to God's words.

An Irrigated Garden

They will come and shout for joy on the heights of Zion; they will be radiant with joy because of the LORD's goodness, because of the grain, the new wine, the fresh oil, and because of the young of the flocks and

herds. Their life will be like an irrigated garden, and they will no longer grow weak from hunger. Jeremiah 31:12

I couldn't stop myself from reading these words over and over again: "Their life will be like an irrigated garden." What a beautiful image of what our lives can look like. I researched the benefits of irrigation, and it's amazing how much they relate to all the benefits and blessings we can experience with God in our hearts.

1.   Irrigation is important because crops should not depend on the rain only.
Like crops, we should not depend on only ourselves if we are going to be successful in patience, forgiveness, grace, courage and faith. Relying only on ourselves will lead to failure, disappointment and won't yield a harvest.

2.   Irrigation allows introduction of high yield crops.
Like irrigation, God can equip and lead us to yield an abundance of fruit (love, patience, kindness, honesty … the best and sweetest fruit of all, the fruits of the spirit).

3.   From the irrigated fields, the yields are stable, reliable and assured production; targets can be met.
With God, who is the same today as He was yesterday and will always be, we can count on a consistent strength and supply of grace, love and forgiveness. We can trust that when He calls us, no matter what He calls us to do, He will equip us with all we need to complete the task.

4.   Irrigation allows for continuous cultivation.
Following God daily and growing in His word gives us a deeper understanding of His heart, ways and desires so that we can follow Him closely in our daily lives while remaining on His righteous path.

5.   Finally, irrigation reduces fluctuations and the risk of crop failure due to drought.

When we focus on the cross, we are less likely to ebb and flow in our hearts and minds. We are less likely to succumb to sinful and selfish desires when we are living close to God and in His word. Please notice I said we are "less likely," not guaranteed. We will falter and fall many times, but with God's grace we can pick ourselves up, dust off and try again.

Overall, there are so many more benefits to living, loving and believing in our faithful Father in Heaven. I don't know about you, but I want my life to be like an irrigated garden that never grows weak or weary, that produces fruit pleasing to our Father and sustains me through the splendor and the desert.

Press Pause

Jeremiah holds so many nuggets of truth. This week, reading Jeremiah's response to the commanders of the armies reminded me of an important practice we often forget when seeking wisdom and direction from the Lord. Let's take a look.

Back then, you hadn't been around long if you hadn't heard of Jeremiah the prophet. So, it wasn't surprising to find the commanders of the armies approaching him to **"hear our petition and pray to the LORD your God for this entire remnant. For as you now see, though we were once many, now only a few are left. Pray that the LORD your God will tell us where we should go and what we should do." Jeremiah 42:2-3**

Like a good prophet, Jeremiah hears their requests and promises to pray for a response and tell them everything the Lord says in response to their request. The commanders even tell Jeremiah that they want to hear the whole truth and nothing but the truth, even if it is unpleasant and not what they want to hear (v. 6). How many times do we pray like this? It's verse seven that caught my attention. **Now at the end of 10 days, the word of the LORD came to Jeremiah. (v. 7)**

First, I'm pretty sure these commanders, in the thick of battle, were hoping for a quick answer. They needed to make some decisions and were relying on hearing from the Lord sooner rather than later. Second, Jeremiah could have just given them his opinion, but he knew better than that. Jeremiah prayed and waited! There is no evidence that shows he knew when the Lord would respond or how many times they may have checked back in with Jeremiah to see if he had heard anything yet, but I would venture to guess the commanders checked in a few times, anxiously awaiting a response and some direction.

Jeremiah waited for ten days until he heard from the Lord! Now, in my book that's a quick turn around, but again they were strategizing and working on battle plans. Both Jeremiah and the commanders waited for the Lord's reply. Jeremiah didn't give his own answer because the Lord didn't answer right away, and the commanders didn't make a move until they heard the word of the Lord from Jeremiah.

This reminded me of how quick I can be to give or take advice before seeking the Lord first. It also reminded me of the times I asked God for direction, got tired of waiting and acted on my own accord (never ending up very well). I know my life, actually all of our lives, would look very different if we could seek the Lord for any and all direction we need, pause until we hear from Him and live out this example to our children and others.

It's a tall order in this world of instant communication, instant grits, popcorn, gratification ... you name it, and we can access it any minute of the day. Will you join me in trying to press the pause button when it comes to our prayer lives and our patience in waiting on the Lord's direction? I'll pray for your strength and courage to attain this goal, and please pray for mine!

AND Then . . . There was Hope

As the book of Jeremiah ends, Lamentations begins. Lamentations are defined as the passionate expression of grief or sorrow; weeping. Moving on to the book of Lamentations, after all the doom and gloom that Isaiah and Jeremiah bestowed on us over the past several weeks, may seem unbearable. With destruction comes grief, sorrow and certainly weeping. However, there is more to this book than just the reminders of misery. As you read through the words, feel the heavy loss and sadness, but pay close attention as you also find hope.

Remember my affliction and my homelessness,
the wormwood and the poison.
I continually remember them
and have become depressed.

Yet I call this to mind,
and therefore I have hope:

Jeremiah speaks of homelessness, poison, depression and wormwood (meaning bitter and detestable). I wonder, how could one sit and remember all the bitterness of his life and still "call to mind hope." Jeremiah knew God's heart, he had witnessed His mighty love, seen His hand in the Master plan and called upon the love He knew God possessed for His people to change his frame of mind.

129

Because of the LORD's faithful love
we do not perish,
for His mercies never end.
They are new every morning;
great is Your faithfulness!
I say: The LORD is my portion,
therefore I will put my hope in Him.

Jeremiah stops in the middle of his mourning to recall the Lord's love, faithfulness and mercies. He remembers that his inheritance is in the Lord. Is it easy or difficult for you to stop in the midst of deep sorrow or trial and remember the truth about our Savior? Personally, I can struggle with keeping this front and center in my heart and thoughts when in the midst of trials, but to grasp and hold onto the fact that our Father's mercies NEVER end and are fresh and new every morning fills my heart with so much hope. Let's keep going.

The LORD is good to those who wait for Him,
to the person who seeks Him.
It is good to wait quietly
for deliverance from the LORD.
It is good for a man to bear the yoke
while he is still young.

Here, Jeremiah points out that God is good to those who seek and wait for Him. As we endure suffering it teaches, molds and strengthens our spirit.

For the Lord
will not reject us forever.
Even if He causes suffering,

**He will show compassion
according to His abundant, faithful love.
For He does not enjoy bringing affliction
or suffering on mankind.
Lamentations 3:19-27, 31-33**

Finally, we see the main reason for hope is that Lord will not reject us forever. God may silence Himself from us for a while and present trying situations for us to learn from, but it will not last forever. Our God has an abundance of love that will override any sorrow or sadness because He does not enjoy bringing affliction on us.

These words from Lamentations describe one of the darkest times for God's people, but we can still glean the lessons of hope it teaches when undergoing suffering. God never changes and has more than enough love, mercy, compassion and faithfulness to overcome any affliction, suffering and hardship we may face. The secret to being able to tap into His mighty love and strength, in the middle of it all, is being able to stop and recognize all God has done and continues to do for us. His compassion never ends and His love endures forever. If we can shift our mindset as Jeremiah shifted his in verses 22-24, then we can find hope in the lamentations.

Today I pray for each person reading this who is experiencing unimaginable suffering, hardship or loss. May God penetrate your heart and show you His everlasting and mighty hope in ways you never imagined could come from your current situation.

Week 35

- ☐ Monday - Ezekiel 1-4
- ☐ Tuesday - Ezekiel 5-8
- ☐ Wednesday - Ezekiel 9-12
- ☐ Thursday - Ezekiel 13-15
- ☐ Friday - Ezekiel 16-17
- ☐ Saturday - Ezekiel 18-19
- ☐ Sunday - Ezekiel 20-21

Week 36

- ☐ Monday - Ezekiel 22-23
- ☐ Tuesday - Ezekiel 24-27
- ☐ Wednesday - Ezekiel 28-31
- ☐ Thursday - Ezekiel 32-34
- ☐ Friday - Ezekiel 35-37
- ☐ Saturday - Ezekiel 38-39
- ☐ Sunday - Ezekiel 40-41

Revelations	
Questions	
Repeats	
Deeper Study	
Etc.	

The Watchman

"I searched for a man among them who would repair the wall and stand in the gap before Me on behalf of the land so that I might not destroy it, but I found no one. So I have poured out My indignation on them and consumed them with the fire of My fury. I have brought their actions down on their own heads." This is the declaration of the LORD God. Ezekiel 22:30-31

"I searched for a man that would stand in the gap before Me." These words kept pouring over and over in my mind as I read Ezekiel. I could not shake them and had to sit for a moment to allow them to soak into my heart. It reminds me of how Moses prayed on behalf of his people for God to be merciful to them despite their complaining and how God promised Abraham he would spare Sodom and Gomorrah if just ten righteous people could be found after his prayers.

Moses and Abraham both stood in the gap for God's broken and wayward people. By doing so, God relented and answered their prayers. As I look back on my life, I'm thankful for the people who have stood in the gap for me during times in my youth when my heart was not with the Lord, or when my mind was so heavy and foggy with grief or pain that I wasn't even able to think clearly.

I've also had the privilege to stand in the gap for friends who were in distress, the hearts of the unsaved in the hope they would come to the Lord and for those I may not have met but have heard their stories. It is heartbreaking to think that the Lord was searching among all men to stand in the gap for Israel but not one was found.

It reminds me of how important it is for each of us to not only pray for our friends and family, but for our country and this world that is so broken. We are quickly falling further and further away from the principles and truths of our Lord and Savior. The foundation our country was founded on has been fractured and is eroding away beneath us. I wonder if God is searching for someone, anyone, out there who will repair the wall and stand in the gap before Him on our behalf. Maybe today is the day we should all ask, "Is it I, Lord?"

 Notes and Reflections:

Week 37

- ☐ Monday - Ezekiel 42-43
- ☐ Tuesday - Ezekiel 44-45
- ☐ Wednesday - Ezekiel 46-48
- ☐ Thursday - Joel 1-3
- ☐ Friday - Daniel 1-3
- ☐ Saturday - Daniel 4-6
- ☐ Sunday - Daniel 7-9

Week 38

- ☐ Monday - Daniel 10-12
- ☐ Tuesday - Ezra 1-3
- ☐ Wednesday - Ezra 4-6; Psalm 137
- ☐ Thursday - Haggai 1-2
- ☐ Friday - Zechariah 1-7
- ☐ Saturday - Zechariah 8-14
- ☐ Sunday - Esther 1-5

Revelations	
Questions	
Repeats	
Deeper Study	
Etc.	

Transmitting Holiness

As Ezekiel was shown vivid visions of the future temple, the Lord said something to him that stopped me once again.

Before they go out to the outer court, to the people, they must take off the clothes they have been ministering in, leave them in the holy chambers, and dress in other clothes so that they do not transmit holiness to the people through their clothes. Ezekiel 44:19

The Lord was explaining that the priests must remove all the clothing they had worn inside the holy chambers, so that when they went out to the people in the courts they wouldn't "transmit holiness" to them. I found this such an interesting concept.

What a great reminder of the privilege it is to serve the Lord in the holy chambers and of how powerful our God truly is. His power and holiness is so great that even the priest's clothes were affected and able to transmit holiness to others who were near.

Although the world may not see us as priests, we are the hands and feet of Christ while He has us on this Earth. We must never forget the sacrifice He made and the privilege it is to serve Him. Unlike the priests of the old covenant, we don't walk in the inner chambers, but we do walk in our homes, communities, churches and neighborhoods. Under the new covenant Jesus left us with the Holy Spirit. So when we are filled and clothed with His Spirit, He wants us to walk among the people and share His holiness, love and grace with others.

Someone recently said, "You have the warmest smile and the nicest aura around you." I had to reply, "Thank you, but it's not me. It's the Holy Spirit." I know without a doubt I'm not capable of a compliment like that unless I'm filled with the Holy Spirit. On my own, I'm not the person I should be or the person who can "transmit" His love to others. How about you? Shall we fill up on the Holy Spirit today and go out and try to transmit a little love into this world? More and more, I've been feeling like this world could use more Jesus.

Even If God Doesn't . . . .

I was thrilled to arrive in the book of Daniel this week! What food for my soul, as I was reminded of the wild and bold faith he held onto through the trials of Babylonian living. Daniel had trusted and honored God's ways and laws in the midst of the toughest of times. He didn't look to the world around him as his guide, but kept his eyes on God. God saw this and honored him throughout his years in Babylon. And what about Daniel's friends Shadrach, Meshach, and Abednego? It is wise to surround yourself with like-minded people and Daniel did just that. Surely, they encouraged one another, for it is easier to stand alongside others than by yourself at times.

When these three were faced with falling down to worship the king and his gods or be burned in the fiery furnace, they chose the furnace. Not only that, they said: **"If the God we serve exists, then He can rescue us from the furnace of blazing fire, and He can rescue us from the power of you, the king. But even if He does not rescue us, we want you as king to know that we will not serve your gods or worship the gold statue you set up." Daniel 3:17-18**

They realized and trusted that God could save them if He chose to; but

139

"even if He didn't," they would not give in and turn away from Him. How many people do you know who haven't gotten what they wanted from God and have turned from Him out of anger, resentment or disgust? I have met quite a few, and it breaks my heart to see what they are missing out on simply because they didn't get what they wanted or thought they deserved. Daniel and his crew realized something that we may tend to forget at times.

Our God is the ... **God who holds your life-breath in His hand and who controls the whole course of your life. Daniel 5:23**

When we allow that to truly sink into our hearts, we will be radically changed and able to trust God more boldly than we ever imagined. I pray as we trust and look to God for direction, that He will honor us with clear answers, blessings and revelations, but even if he doesn't we will praise Him.

No Brainer!

It was so wonderful to find myself back in Zechariah. After writing 30 Days In Zechariah a few years ago, I had moved on to other books and topics in the Bible and not revisited. Yet this prophetic book never ceases to astound me. It's such a beautiful reminder of the God we serve.

A declaration of the LORD,
who stretched out the heavens,
laid the foundation of the earth,
and formed the spirit of man within him. Zechariah 12:1

So often, I hear others say that studying the Bible is difficult to understand and vague. Today, I want to look at two verses tucked into Zechariah that are so clear and concise there is no way around their meaning and the intention the Lord has set for us to follow.

These are the things you must do: Speak truth to one another; make true and sound decisions within your gates. Do not plot evil in your hearts against your neighbor, and do not love perjury, for I hate all this—this is the LORD's declaration. Zechariah 8:16-17

Those of you who have read my books and blog know I'm a Type A personality. I love a list and I love to cross things off my list as I accomplish them. God doesn't usually set a list before us … so when He does, I grab it. This is a very concise list and the Lord is very clear about our "must dos" and what He "hates."

We must: speak the truth and make true (real or genuine) and sound decisions.

We must not: plot evil against others or love perjury (breaking an oath and lying).

The Lord is sharing this "list" with Zechariah in a vision and promising that He will bring His people back to Jerusalem once again. **For the LORD of Hosts says this: "As I resolved to treat you badly when your fathers provoked Me to anger, and I did not relent," says the LORD of Hosts, "so I have resolved again in these days to do what is good to Jerusalem and the house of Judah. Don't be afraid (Zechariah 8:14-15).**

The Lord promised to bless His people once again and was encouraging them not to be afraid about provoking Him. Just speak truth and make genuine decisions, don't plot evil and break your oaths, the Lord explains, and you will be fine.

141

Honestly, it boils down to those things for each of us. Think about how those two "dos" and two "do-nots" encompass all the Ten Commandments and could guide our actions, words and deeds every day of our lives. If we could just get these four things down with a bit more precision, our lives would be on a track to live life in a closer walk with our Heavenly Father.

Stay strong ... there are only four more weeks of Old Testament and then we will finally be in the New Testament! It's been so much fun to discover all the nuggets of truth and wisdom tucked into the OT, but *I'm ready for some Jesus after all this exile! How about you?*

 Notes and Reflections:

Week 39

- ☐ Monday - Esther 6-10
- ☐ Tuesday - Ezra 7-10
- ☐ Wednesday - Nehemiah 1-5
- ☐ Thursday - Nehemiah 6-7
- ☐ Friday - Nehemiah 8-10
- ☐ Saturday - Nehemiah 11-13; Psalm 126
- ☐ Sunday - Malachi 1-4

Week 40

- ☐ Monday - Luke 1; John 1:1-14
- ☐ Tuesday - Matthew 1; Luke 2:1-38
- ☐ Wednesday - Matthew 2; Luke 2:39-52
- ☐ Thursday - Matthew 3; Mark 1; Luke 3
- ☐ Friday - Matthew 4; Luke 4-5; John 1:15-51
- ☐ Saturday - John 2-4
- ☐ Sunday - Mark 2

Revelations	
Questions	
Repeats	
Deeper Study	
Etc.	

A Record of Wrongs

While Ezra prayed and confessed, weeping and falling facedown before the house of God, an extremely large assembly of Israelite men, women, and children gathered around him. The people also wept bitterly. Then Shecaniah son of Jehiel, an Elamite, responded to Ezra: "We have been unfaithful to our God by marrying foreign women from the surrounding peoples, but there is still hope for Israel in spite of this. Let us therefore make a covenant before our God to send away all the foreign wives and their children, according to the counsel of my LORD and of those who tremble at the command of our God. Let it be done according to the law. Get up, for this matter is your responsibility, and we support you. Be strong and take action!" Ezra 10:1-4

Ezra and his fellow exiles investigated all the families and found anyone who had gone against the Lord's declaration by marrying foreign women. I don't blame them for going through things with a fine tooth comb. They had suffered enough in exile and were finally trying to get back to the doing the right thing so they could "avert the fierce anger of God" in this matter and any other (v.14).

The following were found to have married foreign women from the descendants of the priests: from the descendants of Jeshua son of Jozadak and his brothers: Maaseiah, Eliezer, Jarib, and Gedaliah. Ezra 10:18

The list of offenders continues through verse 43! Check it out. What struck me about this passage was that every offender and their descendants are listed out and in the Bible. It's one thing to be in the news feed for a few days after a scuffle or indiscretion, but can you imagine having your sins and name listed out in the most read book of all time?

Pondering this, I realized that too often our sins are hidden away, out of sight and tucked in our hearts, so it's easy to overlook them and move on. If we knew all our sins would be listed out in the Bible, or even tomorrow's news feed, we might take a closer look at our actions, words and deeds throughout the day. We might think twice before giving in to sin. In fact, we might go to God on a more regular basis for forgiveness and strength to do the right thing so we can avoid the sin all together.

Even though our sins aren't written out in the Bible, God knows every one of them and desires to clean the slate or wipe the page if go to Him and ask. Just ask! No special form, no fee and no hoops to jump through. Just ask and He will wipe the page clean for you.

How fitting that just yesterday we celebrated Easter and a Risen Savior. The one who died on the cross to cover all those nasty sins and start a new covenant with our Lord. This week ends our journey through the Old Testament and begins our adventures in the New Testament. What an awesome way to begin the New Testament as we read and study more about the Son of God who made forgiveness and eternal life for us possible with the blood He shed for us.

Out of the Blue?

I can't tell you how incredible it was to read through the Old Testament in chronological order. God opened my eyes to abundantly more than I could have hoped. However, I am so very grateful to be moving on to the New Testament this week. Glory! I appreciated Jesus and His sacrifice before, but today I can honestly say I have a greater and deeper appreciation for Him than ever before. This year's journey is changing my heart to look more like His and showing me the great power of His word in ways I've never known. That said, let's get into some Gospels!

The beginning of Luke reminds us this book was a letter to Theophilus. We don't know anything about Theophilus except the book of Acts was also a letter written to him. Even though it's thought that Luke was written after both Matthew and Mark, I pause on his book today because Luke was an avid researcher and Gentile. He didn't take the stories of Jesus lightly and investigated them in detail before compiling his letter.

Many have undertaken to compile a narrative about the events that have been fulfilled among us, just as the original eyewitnesses and servants of the word handed them down to us. It also seemed good to me, since I have carefully investigated everything from the very first, to write to you in an orderly sequence, most honorable Theophilus, so that you may know the certainty of the things about which you have been instructed. Luke 1:1-4

In fact, without the book of Luke we wouldn't know as much as we do about the life of Jesus. Scholars have even said that almost 60% of Luke isn't even mentioned in the other gospels (HCSB, pg. 1725). Unique to Luke is information on the births of John the Baptist and Jesus, more detailed travel information, the Emmaus road experience, the only description of Jesus' ascension into Heaven and much more. For me, this illustrates the obsession Luke had for research and detail.

Many of us know John the Baptist's story of being born to Elizabeth, who was too old to conceive, after an angel appeared to her husband in the temple. You may also remember how John the Baptist leapt in Elizabeth's womb when Mary, who was pregnant with Jesus, came to visit. All that information really stands out, but I came across this little nugget about John the Baptist that particularly caught my eye.

The child grew up and became spiritually strong, and he was in the wilderness until the day of his public appearance to Israel. Luke 1:80

John was clearly sent by God to foretell of the coming of Jesus. God ensured his parents (although old) had a firm foundation and clearly brought him up under God's laws, but they were old, so either they died and left John, they couldn't keep up with him because of their age so he roamed the wilderness or he preferred the wilderness. Whatever the case, what's amazing to me is that He stayed tucked away out of the public eye only to step out at the age of 30 and begin a very public ministry foretelling of the Savior of the world and Son of God.

Wow! Think about it. He went from wilderness to the spotlight overnight. If you ever doubt that God can take your set of skills (no matter how insignificant they seem to you) and use them for His glory, I pray you will remember John the Baptist. If you ever feel as if you don't have enough experience or God doesn't have a plan for your life, I pray you will remember John the Baptist. I wonder how John finally realized his role for God's Kingdom? What made him set out at the age of 30 to begin telling others about Jesus? These and so many more questions keep me coming back to God's story daily.

Gone Fishing

As He was passing along by the Sea of Galilee, He saw Simon and Andrew, Simon's brother. They were casting a net into the sea, since they were fishermen. "Follow Me," Jesus told them, "and I will make you fish for people!" [18] Immediately they left their nets and followed Him. Mark 1:16-18

As I read the verses above from Mark, I wondered what had happened for Simon and Andrew to immediately leave their families and jobs to follow Jesus. Had John the Baptist told them Jesus was coming or did they have an overwhelming desire in their hearts to follow Jesus because God was leading them? Then, I get to Luke and find all the answers. Read Luke 5:1-11.

Luke gives us the rest of the story. Not only was Jesus along the lake teaching, He specifically picked out Simon to show him a clear sign (or miracle) that He was who He said He was (the Son of God). This had such an effect on Simon that he immediately felt his sin and unworthiness, falling to his knees before the Lord. And I love how Jesus says, just as the angels all through the Bible told prophet after prophet and then Mary, "Don't be afraid."

The power of these three words from our Father in Heaven is tremendous. Let's sit on them for just a minute. What if you came to your Father in prayer daily and remembered what He is whispering to your heart?

Don't be afraid, I will accept your apology and forgive you no matter what the sin. Don't be afraid, the price for your sin was paid when my

Son died on the cross so that you could receive eternal life. Don't be afraid, I created you, adore you and only want to draw you closer to me. Don't be afraid, I already know your heart, there is nothing you can hide from me. Don't be afraid, I know you are struggling with that sin and I desire to help you if you will just ask. Don't be afraid, even when you don't feel me close, I'm walking beside you. Don't be afraid, my plan is perfect and you are a part of it. Don't be afraid, there is no sin too big for me to handle and heal you from, if you allow Me in. Don't be afraid, I will guide and protect you with my strong Hand.

I could go on and on because when you know God through the reading of His word, you know Him personally and His promises to be true. If we could remember to place fear aside, I feel strongly we would run to our Lord and Savior "immediately." We would serve, follow, listen and allow Him to guide us always and respond immediately to His request and nudge.

I pray as we each go throughout the week we will reflect and ponder what it is we are afraid of when it comes to our Father in Heaven. Is it a fear of forgiveness, acceptance, loss of control or something else? If we can identify the fear, allow God to remove it and heal us, our trust, desire to follow Him and peace will follow.

 Notes and Reflections:

Week 41

- ☐ Monday - John 5
- ☐ Tuesday - Matthew 12:1-21; Mark 3; Luke 6
- ☐ Wednesday - Matthew 5-7
- ☐ Thursday - Matthew 8:1-13; Luke 7
- ☐ Friday - Matthew 11
- ☐ Saturday - Matthew 12:22-50; Luke 11
- ☐ Sunday - Matthew 13; Luke 8

Week 42

- ☐ Monday - Matthew 8:14-34; Mark 4-5
- ☐ Tuesday - Matthew 9-10
- ☐ Wednesday - Matthew 14; Mark 6; Luke 9:1-17
- ☐ Thursday - John 6
- ☐ Friday - Matthew 15; Mark 7
- ☐ Saturday - Matthew 16; Mark 8; Luke 9:18-27
- ☐ Sunday - Matthew 17; Mark 9; Luke 9:28-62

Revelations	
Questions	
Repeats	
Deeper Study	
Etc.	

Do Not Be AMAZED!

These four words caught my eye as I read John 3-5. Jesus uses them before two important teaching points concerning the Lord's return and our eternal life with Him in Heaven.

Do not be amazed that I told you that you must be born again. John 3:7

Do not be amazed at this, because a time is coming when all who are in the graves will hear His voice. John 5:28

As I re-read Jesus' Sermon on the Mount in Matthew 5-7 from Matthew's perspective, I was reminded how countercultural and full of love and grace Jesus was (and is). As you read through the following verses, try to imagine sitting on a beautiful mountainside, looking up at the Son of God and hearing Him speak these words to your heart. Imagine the spectacular glory of the backdrop and basking in the Son of God's presence. Although you may not be sitting on the mountainside as you read this, you are hearing the words our Savior spoke.

You are the light of the world. A city situated on a hill cannot be hidden. No one lights a lamp and puts it under a basket, but rather on a lampstand, and it gives light for all who are in the house. In the same way, let your light shine before men, so that they may see your good works and give glory to your Father in heaven (Matthew 5:14-16)·

If we are to be the light of the world, these instructions are vital to keeping our light shining in the darkness of this world.

- Murder and Adultery don't just include actions, the thought and the words make you guilty as well (v.21-28).

- **It was also said, Whoever divorces his wife must give her a written notice of divorce. But I tell you, everyone who divorces his wife, except in a case of sexual immorality, causes her to commit adultery. And whoever marries a divorced woman commits adultery (v. 31-32).**

- Don't swear or take oaths, just be true to your word. **Let your word 'yes' be 'yes,' and your 'no' be 'no.' Anything more than this is from the evil one** (v. 33-35, 36-38).

- Don't repay evil with evil, but instead look away and pray for your enemy. Not just those whom you love, but also those you hate (v. 38-45).

- Give, pray and fast in private. Don't do it to show off, but for the Lord and you will be rewarded (Matthew 6:1-6).

- Don't worry yourself with earthly money and treasures, but store up treasures and memories of the heart because they can't be stolen or rust away. You can't love your God above all else when money and possessions have made you a slave to them (v. 19-24).

- You are worth more to God than any bird or sunflower and He provides for them. So don't worry about tomorrow or the next day, but instead focus your attention on the present and the provision that God has given you for that day and moment (v. 25-34).

- Don't be so judgmental. Instead of worrying about your neighbor's trash – take our your own and then you can help him with his (Matthew 7:1-6).

- Please ask Me [God] for help. If you ask Me, seek My wisdom and knock on My door, I will open it and give you more than you ever imagined. If I don't answer the first time, don't give up! (v. 7-12).

- The world loves to take the easy way, but the way to Me is through the teeny, tiny narrow gate that so few find and then are willing to enter. Don't follow the herd, follow Me. It isn't easy and it takes time, courage and dedication, but the reward will be great (v. 13-23).

- Build your life, your values, morals and heart upon My word because it is the strongest foundation available. I promise you, not matter what else you try will only end in complete disaster and destruction

I paraphrased these with my simple words, but w**hen Jesus had finished this sermon, the crowds were astonished at His teaching, because He was teaching them like one who had authority, and not like their scribes. Matthew 6:28-29**

I pray these reminders will sink into our hearts and renew our desire to follow Jesus and be His light in this dark world.

Five Random Things

Soon afterward He was traveling from one town and village to another, preaching and telling the good news of the kingdom of God. The Twelve were with Him, and also some women who had been healed of evil spirits and sicknesses: Mary, called Magdalene (seven demons had come out of her); Joanna the wife of Chuza, Herod's steward; Susanna; and many others who were supporting them from their possessions. Luke 8:1-3

1. I adore how Jesus had so many women with Him and the disciples as they traveled to share good news and heal the sick. This wasn't just a fraternity or man's work. I always knew that Mary Magdalen adored Jesus and was special to Him. However, reading Luke reminded me that any woman who had been possessed by seven demons and cured would surely follow the one who saved her — and we know who that was! Can you imagine it? Her faith, adoration and love had been earned in a very special way, and she never forgot all Jesus did for her. Sometimes I feel like I forget the blessings God pours out on me and my family as time moves on, but Mary Magdalene didn't and I don't want to either.

When He had come to the other side, to the region of the Gadarenes, two demon-possessed men met Him as they came out of the tombs. They were so violent that no one could pass that way. Suddenly they shouted, "What do You have to do with us, Son of God? Have You come here to torment us before the time?" Matthew 8:28-29

2. The demons recognized Jesus over everyone else. This reminded me that when we are more like Pharisees (more focused on self, man-made rules and pride) we can miss the incredible presence of God that is right before us. Unlike the demons, Jesus isn't around to torment us, but to love, cherish, forgive and adore. I don't know about you, but I can always use a little more of that.

Jesus sent out these 12 after giving them instructions: "Don't take the road leading to other nations, and don't enter any Samaritan town. Instead, go to the lost sheep of the house of Israel. As you go, announce this: 'The kingdom of heaven has come near.' Matthew 10:5-7

3. "This kingdom of heaven has come near." There have been a few times I can distinctly remember the "kingdom coming near." They are indescribable moments I treasure and have tucked away in my heart as Mary did when Jesus was born. However, I wonder how many times the kingdom has come near to me, but I have missed it due to sin, distractions and selfishness? I desire to know each and every time the kingdom comes near to me, and I pray we will all begin to recognize it over the noise of the world.

Nothing that goes into a person from outside can defile him, but the things that come out of a person are what defile him. [If anyone has ears to hear, he should listen!]" Mark 7:15-16

4. Like many others, I am constantly counting the grams of sugar, fat, carbs and calories of everything I put into my mouth. Jesus' words here brought great conviction to my spirit. What if I paused, read the label (thought about what I was about to say before speaking) and considered it along with everything else I had eaten that day (looked at the long-term effects) before I opened my mouth to speak each time? If I spent as much time decoding my words and heart as I did my food labels, my relationships would probably be much healthier.

When the disciples asked Jesus why they couldn't drive the demon out of a man, he replied, **"Because of your little faith," He told them. "For I assure you: If you have faith the size of a mustard seed, you will tell this mountain, 'Move from here to there,' and it will move. Nothing will be impossible for you. [However, this kind does not come out except by prayer and fasting.]" Matthew 17:20-21**

5. This verse is used a lot on bookmarks, stickers and pictures, but
    sometimes when verses are used this much, I tend to overlook
    the significance of them. As I read it this week, I was reminded
    that God doesn't require us to have faith the size of Montana.
    He doesn't need more from us, He just needs us to come as we
    are. We don't need to be perfect or have everything in order.
    The irony is that we are only made perfect through Him, and He
    will place everything in the correct order if we seek Him with
    just the tiniest size of faith.

These five thoughts are just the tip of the iceberg. Jesus said so much
that we need to consider, discover and reflect on, but we can't do that
until we pick up His word. There is no better way to discover who God is
and what His promises are.

    Notes and Reflections:

Week 43

- ☐ Monday - Matthew 18
- ☐ Tuesday - John 7-8
- ☐ Wednesday - John 9; John 10:1-21
- ☐ Thursday - Luke 10; John 10:22-42
- ☐ Friday - Luke 12-13
- ☐ Saturday - Luke 14-15
- ☐ Sunday - Luke 16; Luke 17:1-10

Week 44

- ☐ Monday - John 11
- ☐ Tuesday - Luke 17:11-37; Luke 18:1-14
- ☐ Wednesday - Matthew 19; Mark 10
- ☐ Thursday - Matthew 20-21
- ☐ Friday - Luke 18:15--43; Luke 19
- ☐ Saturday - Mark 11; John 12
- ☐ Sunday - Matthew 22; Mark 12

Revelations	
Questions	
Repeats	
Deeper Study	
Etc.	

Not an easy path, but a clear one!

Do you really have to believe in Jesus to get to Heaven?

I've always been passionate about sharing the importance of reading scripture for yourself, so that you will know and trust the promises and truths God has for us. I've said many times before, I was late in my understanding and faith in these promises because I listened to what everyone else said about God and His Word and didn't dig into the Bible for myself until later in life. It's difficult to gain the trust of a friend of a friend, but not a personal friend. This is one huge benefit of reading/studying scripture for ourselves. We get to know God, our trust grows deeper and we realize who we are in Him.

So Jesus said to the Jews who had believed Him, "If you continue in My word, you really are My disciples. You will know the truth, and the truth will set you free." John 8:31-32

Reading scripture doesn't just solidify our faith and help us recognize Him. It also clarifies everything the world does such a great job muddying up for us. I will admit to once having wavering and fence-sitting opinions on many issues such as abortion, marriage, eternal life and creation until I opened the Word of God and read it myself.

When he has brought all his own outside, he goes ahead of them. The sheep follow him because they recognize his voice. They will never follow a stranger; instead they will run away from him, because they don't recognize the voice of strangers. John 10:4-5

The best part of knowing and reading God's Word is that it's full of truth and clarity, which leads to a clear path to travel. Not an easy path, but a clear path. To read His word is to know Him, His laws and His ways. It is very easy to be deceived by others, this world and Satan when we are not clear on who God is and what He calls sin. I fell victim to this gray watered-down syndrome for years because I only listened to what others said about God.

One Sabbath, when He went to eat at the house of one of the leading Pharisees, they were watching Him closely. There in front of Him was a man whose body was swollen with fluid. In response, Jesus asked the law experts and the Pharisees, "Is it lawful to heal on the Sabbath or not?" But they kept silent. He took the man, healed him, and sent him away. And to them, He said, "Which of you whose son or ox falls into a well, will not immediately pull him out on the Sabbath day?" To this they could find no answer. Luke 14:1-6

It's vital to know and understand God's ways and laws. Just as the Pharisees where watching Jesus closely to see what He would do, others are watching us each and every day. When we call ourselves Christians, others are looking at us more closely than anyone else to see how we respond, what we believe and how we react. We don't have to live in the gray of this world that will ebb and flow like the tides. The strength, clarity, peace, strength and truth we desire are all sitting on the bookshelf in the book we call the Bible. The question is, will we pick it up?

Just the Facts, Please!

There are many stories within the New Testament that I've heard or read over and over again. Many of Jesus' parables stand out and are often used in messages and Bible studies. However, this week in Luke I ran across a parable called the rich man and Lazarus. I seldom hear it mentioned or taught on. I encourage you to read it in its entirety. It

162

doesn't need any explanation and speaks for itself in very convicting way.

Read Luke 16:19-31. No commentary needed, right? So how about a prayer.

God, may our hearts and minds be open to receiving your Word. Give us the strength and the courage to share the good news of eternal life through your Son, Jesus Christ so that others may know You. Increase our faith to levels we could have never anticipated or expected, so that we can remain under Your wing and receive the gift of eternal life through the sacrifice of Jesus on the cross. In Your name we pray, Amen.

Hangry!?

Hangry! It's a combination of the words hungry and angry. We commonly use this term at our house when our daughter hasn't eaten, because when she is hungry her temper is quick to ignite and her patience is nonexistent. Like many of us, she responds more reasonably when her stomach isn't growling. It occurred to me as I read Mark 11 that Jesus may have had suffered a case of being "hangry" while He walked this Earth in human form.

The next day when they came out from Bethany, He was hungry. After seeing in the distance a fig tree with leaves, He went to find out if there was anything on it. When He came to it, He found nothing but leaves, because it was not the season for figs. He said to it, "May no one ever eat fruit from you again!" And His disciples heard it. They

came to Jerusalem, and He went into the temple complex and began to throw out those buying and selling in the temple. He overturned the money changers' tables and the chairs of those selling doves, and would not permit anyone to carry goods through the temple complex. Mark 11:12-16

The withering of the fig tree is the only miracle of destruction recorded in the Gospels. Throughout the Old Testament the fig tree is used to symbolize Israel. Jesus used this illustration to teach the disciples a lesson about faith, but I wonder if I started out as a lesson or was just reaction to a moment of intense hunger (Mark 11:20-26). Jesus was, after all, human when He walked this Earth. As the Son of God, He had access to the Father, but He was flesh and bones and suffered from hunger. I think He may have had a moment of "hangry" here as He approached the fig tree in the hopes of nourishment. Finding nothing but leaves left Him a bit miffed, and He responded by cursing the fig tree.

Then the scriptures move right into His exchange and tossing of tables in the temple complex. I don't know how much time had passed from the moment of cursing the fig tree to the temple, but Bethany is only two miles from Jerusalem (the temple). It would seem He left Bethany hungry and not getting anything from the fig tree, He arrived at the temple in Jerusalem hungry and agitated.

No doubt Jesus was disturbed and angered by the "den of thieves" that were defiling His Father's house, but I always thought it was a bit uncharacteristic of Him to come through tossing tables when He usually offered up a parable (v. 17).

164

Was Jesus just "hangry"? This would make cursing the fig tree and tossing the tables at the temple understandable. I don't know, but it's fun to ponder. It's interesting to consider the complexities He must have faced as the Son of God walking around in human form. This is what's so exciting about reading the Bible. There is always a new bit of information to consider. Truly, we serve an amazing God! One who has such a great sense of love for us He sent His son to walk among us so He could relate to and understand the temptations we face in this flawed flesh.

 Notes and Reflections:

Week 45

- ☐ Monday - Matthew 23; Luke 20-21
- ☐ Tuesday - Mark 13
- ☐ Wednesday - Matthew 24
- ☐ Thursday - Matthew 25
- ☐ Friday - Matthew 26; Mark 14
- ☐ Saturday - Luke 22; John 13
- ☐ Sunday - John 14-17

Week 46

- ☐ Monday - Matthew 27; Mark 15
- ☐ Tuesday - Luke 23; John 18-19
- ☐ Wednesday - Matthew 28; Mark 16
- ☐ Thursday - Luke 24; John 20-21
- ☐ Friday - Acts 1-3
- ☐ Saturday - Acts 4-6
- ☐ Sunday - Acts 7-8

Revelations	
Questions	
Repeats	
Deeper Study	
Etc.	

At All Times

Jesus spends a lot of time explaining the end of time and God's return to His disciples. I'm so thankful it's included in the gospels. I have studied more of the end times prophesy in Daniel, Zechariah and Revelation this year than ever before. I found it so interesting to sit and savor these words Jesus spoke about His glorious return. The story of the ten virgins is a parable that doesn't get mentioned in messages/sermons much. I had never read it so closely and considered its implications.

Read Matthew 25:1-13.

I do not want to be caught off guard when the Savior returns. Matthew reminds us in chapter 24 that Christ's return will be like the days of Noah and Sodom and Gomorrah when everyone was going about their daily business of working, getting married, eating and drinking. All of a sudden, the flood hits and the city fell. Except for a few, no one was ready because they had not read the scriptures and noticed the warning signs that were given by prophets and angels.

Although God is the only one who knows the exact day and time He will return (Matthew 24:36), we have the scriptures and words that Jesus and other prophets have left us to open our eyes to the signs of His return. We must read, know and consider what it means to be ready *at all times* for His return. As Luke says,

"Be on your guard, so that your minds are not dulled from carousing, drunkenness, and worries of life, or that day will come on you unexpectedly like a trap. For it will come on all who live on the face of the whole earth. But be alert at all times, praying that you may have

strength to escape all these things that are going to take place and to stand before the Son of Man." Luke 21:34-36

Still Remaining

Each year I choose a word to dwell on during the year that the Lord usually places on my heart. This time that word was, "remain." Over and over again, this was a word He continually placed in my path. You can read more about this from my blog post titled The Year of Remain at https://thewhisperofgod.wordpress.com/2015/03/16/the-year-of-remain/.

As I get closer to the end of this chronological Bible journey, it was the sweetest blessing to find, tucked into John 15, a reminder of why I have done this and how much I have grown over the past year simply by remaining in God and His word.

Remain in Me, and I in you. Just as a branch is unable to produce fruit by itself unless it remains on the vine, so neither can you unless you remain in Me. (v. 4)

If you remain in Me and My words remain in you, ask whatever you want and it will be done for you. (v. 7)

As the Father has loved Me, I have also loved you. Remain in My love. If you keep My commands you will remain in My love, just as I have kept My Father's commands and remain in His love. (v. 9-10)

Tears well up in my eyes as I type this and consider all the benefits we receive by simply remaining in the light of our Heavenly Father's word. There are many of us who never make the time, think we are too busy, that it's a waste of time, that it isn't relevant anymore or that we can't understand what it means, so what's the point. I remember using a few of these same excuses years ago. Please don't assume what others say about the Bible is true. Read it for yourself and know it's a face to face conversation with your Heavenly Father that He so desperately wants to have with you. If our favorite movie star or athlete called to say they wanted to meet for dinner, I have no doubt most of us would take out a loan for the flight, drop everything and rearrange our schedules to get there. Well, the Creator of the Universe wants to have a one-on-one with you. The Creator of everything that has ever been and will ever be. Will you meet Him?

We have access to knowledge, wisdom and understanding that we can only begin to tap into and comprehend when we read the Bible. As Jesus said in John 16:1, **"I have told you these things to keep you from stumbling."** I pray each of us will carve out the time the study God's word, that we would thirst for Him in new ways and that He will create a fire in our hearts to remain in Him today and every day of our lives.

KEEP IT UP!

In Matthew 26 we find Jesus in the Garden of Gethsemane with His disciples before His arrest and crucifixion. He understands what's at stake and what's coming. Jesus knows the Father's will and the part He is to play in the divine plan. Unlike many from other countries, we don't find ourselves faced with life and death situations often. However, when we are in the midst of great trial, persecution and pain, we tend to lean on God closely through prayer. Often, we will even ask others to come alongside us and pray for us as well.

Jesus spent His life and ministry living and loving in the way He desired for us to live and love. Where we find Him at the end of His ministry is no different.

After leaving them, He went away again and prayed a third time, saying the same thing once more. Matthew 26:44

Jesus kept coming back after prayer to His disciples, whom He had asked to stay awake and pray for Him, only to find them asleep. This was a gentle reminder to me that my strength can't and won't come from others or from myself, but must come from the Lord. Not only that, Jesus shows us that fear can be overcome with prayer, and faith in the Father is essential to living out our lives for His glory.

Even Jesus, as He told us to do in Matthew 7:7, prayed without ceasing and was not afraid to go before God three times and ask for the same thing once more. Jesus wanted God to answer His prayer and allow His fate on the cross to be overturned. Jesus knew at the mere whisper of a word that God could send His legions of angels to rescue Him, but He also trusted God and loved Him enough to follow His plan and trust the path set before Him.

I will never forget when God called me to writing and speaking. I was, and always had been, terrified of public speaking. I truly am living proof that when He calls you to do something, He equips you with what you need to carry out His will. As I sat in prayer one day before my first speaking event, God spoke straight to my heart and whispered, "Allison, I don't need you to go out on that stage and be nailed to the cross. I've already taken care of that. I just need you to go out there and share the story of how I have worked in your life. Can you do that?" I wasn't facing a life and death situation, but my fear was so strong it felt as serious. I prayed, I prayed over and over and then I trusted when He said, "Go!" Since that day I took that first step of faith in this journey, God has never let me down and always showed up with His strength.

Is there something in your life that the Lord is calling you to do that you have put aside because it was too scary, didn't make sense or you felt like you didn't have the abilities necessary? Pray, and pray again. Ask God what His will is, but be ready to accept and move forward when He whispers, "Not your will, but Mine. Will you trust and follow Me?"

The BIG Turnaround

At that time Jesus said to the crowds, "Have you come out with swords and clubs, as if I were a criminal, to capture Me? Every day I used to sit, teaching in the temple complex, and you didn't arrest Me. But all this has happened so that the prophetic Scriptures would be fulfilled." Then all the disciples deserted Him and ran away. Matthew 26:55-56

We are the only religion that serves a risen God. No other religion can claim this, but how do we know for sure? If your faith isn't quite big enough to trust and believe the scriptures, take a look at a few human men in history that show us seeing is believing.

After Jesus was arrested in the Garden of Gethsemane, we read above in Matthew 26 that "all the disciples deserted Him and ran away." They hit the road, denied knowing Him and went back to their old fishing jobs

172

(John 21). They may have even felt a little stupid. They had given up everything (lives, families, jobs) and followed this man called Jesus for three years thinking He was the Messiah, the Son of God who would save the world and now He was dead. But then something happened ... something so amazing ... something so big that even when the high priests and elders ordered the disciples to stop telling the story of Jesus, they were unable to "stop speaking about what they had seen and heard." They suffered floggings, ridicule, death threats and prison.

So they called for them and ordered them not to preach or teach at all in the name of Jesus. But Peter and John answered them, "Whether it's right in the sight of God for us to listen to you rather than to God, you decide; for we are unable to stop speaking about what we have seen and heard." Acts 4:18-20

After they called in the apostles and had them flogged, they ordered them not to speak in the name of Jesus and released them. Then they went out from the presence of the Sanhedrin, rejoicing that they were counted worthy to be dishonored on behalf of the Name. Every day in the temple complex, and in various homes, they continued teaching and proclaiming the good news that Jesus is the Messiah. Acts 5:40-42

Why would anyone put their life on the line to tell a story that wasn't true? They wouldn't. Maybe one of them was crazy, but not all of them. Jesus really did rise after three days. He even ate, hung out with and presented Himself to Mary and His disciples several times, before ascending into Heaven to sit at the right hand of God the Father.

After He had suffered, He also presented Himself alive to them by many convincing proofs, appearing to them during 40 days and speaking about the kingdom of God. Acts 1:3

Can you imagine living to see and share a story like this? The biggest story in all of history! How could you keep that under wraps? I'm so thankful God knew what it would take to grab the hearts and trust of our faulty human minds and hearts. His plan is a miraculous and amazing one that leaves me sitting here in awe of His love for each of us and in gratitude for those who shared boldly and loudly the good news that Jesus is the Messiah. I pray we can be as bold as Jesus's disciples and share the story of our risen Savior that will return for us once again.

 Notes and Reflections:

Week 47

- ☐ Monday - Acts 9-10
- ☐ Tuesday - Acts 11-12
- ☐ Wednesday - Acts 13-14
- ☐ Thursday - James 1-5
- ☐ Friday - Acts 15-16
- ☐ Saturday - Galatians 1-3
- ☐ Sunday - Galatians 4-6

Week 48

- ☐ Monday - Acts 17; Acts 18:1-18
- ☐ Tuesday - 1 Thessalonians 1-5; 2 Thessalonians 1-3
- ☐ Wednesday - Acts 18:19-28; Acts 19
- ☐ Thursday - 1 Corinthians 1-4
- ☐ Friday - 1 Corinthians 5-8
- ☐ Saturday - 1 Corinthians 9-11
- ☐ Sunday - 1 Corinthians 12-14

Revelations	
Questions	
Repeats	
Deeper Study	
Etc.	

Another Gospel

As I read Paul's letter to the church of Galatia, I was only a few lines in when his words hit home.

I am amazed that you are so quickly turning away from Him who called you by the grace of Christ and are turning to a different gospel— not that there is another gospel, but there are some who are troubling you and want to change the good news about the Messiah. But even if we or an angel from heaven should preach to you a gospel other than what we have preached to you, a curse be on him! Galatians 1:6-8

I was so convicted by these three verses of scripture I had to pause and pray for myself, my family and this nation. After all we know to be true about our Savior and King, after all the times we have seen Him at work in our lives and the lives of others, after all the moments of divine meetings and answered prayers ... How can we be so quick to turn from Him?

We can so easily fall into the trap of following "another gospel." The gospel of the world brings fear, pride, selfishness, greed, anger, discontentment, materialism and sexual immorality and sets it up on an altar before us. This world casts a wide net that can trap us into believing in something more than our Savior. I pray we don't forget that we will NEVER fit into this world because this is not our home. When we feel left out, alone and strange for not worshiping these modern-day idols, we have to remind ourselves and fellow brothers and sisters in Christ that the narrow gate is difficult to find and tricky to fit through. It takes work, dedication and commitment, but the benefits that the one true God has promised us are worth every second of those feelings. Uncomfortable is a good thing!

My prayer is that we are not quickly distracted by the shiny and temporary things of this world. May we always have the cross before us as we honor and worship the One who has called us by the grace of Christ.

Manager of Mysteries

Recently a friend of mine shared about a conversation he had with another friend concerning the unhappiness he felt in his life. My friend told him, "The problem is that you have put God in a box. You have decided who God is, without considering who the Bible says He is. You are so busy telling God what you want that you aren't trusting God and allowing Him to work."

As I continued my adventures through Acts, Thessalonians and Corinthians I discovered several reminders of the remarkable God we serve and couldn't help but take some time to highlight them and expand on just a few that stood out to me.

The people here were more open-minded than those in Thessalonica, since they welcomed the message with eagerness and examined the Scriptures daily to see if these things were so. Consequently, many of them believed, including a number of the prominent Greek women as well as men. Acts 17:11-12

Our Father knew we would struggle with faith and trust in His ways and wonders. He knew, and Jesus experienced, the temptation of sin we would face while we walk in this flesh. So, He made sure we had the most effective, loving and complete story of His ways, His love and His laws. A "life's little instruction" book to refer to and live by. The trick is that we must open this book with "eagerness and examine the scriptures" as the early believers did. After all, it tells us many things about our spectacular God! Our **God who made the world and everything in it—He is LORD of heaven and earth and does not live in shrines made by hands (Acts 17:24).**

For the mystery of lawlessness is already at work, but the one now restraining will do so until he is out of the way, and then the lawless one will be revealed. The LORD Jesus will destroy him with the breath of His mouth and will bring him to nothing with the brightness of His coming. 2 Thessalonians 2:7-8

Not only did our amazing and loving Creator leave us with an instruction manual and history of our faith, He left us with a book that describes the strength, character and power our Father has. One day, the Creator and Giver of Life will destroy the lawless one (Satan) with only the breath of His mouth. He created life with His breath and He will end the roaming of Satan the same way. We serve a God who doesn't even have to lift a finger to defeat our enemies. I'm proud to call my Savior the God of angel armies.

What then is Apollos? And what is Paul? They are servants through whom you believed, and each has the role the LORD has given. I planted, Apollos watered, but God gave the growth. 1 Corinthians 3:5-6

We serve a God who doesn't require *everything* of us. Who loves us because we believe in His Son Jesus Christ and His sacrifice. Nothing we can do will make Him love us more, because in Christ He already adores us more than we can fathom. We each have a role to play in His kingdom, gifts He has given us and people He places in our lives so we

179

can share Christ, but He gives the growth. He gives the gifts. He gives the opportunities. He is sovereign and is the ultimate care giver. If we will allow Him to work within us, He will make a way and provide the opportunities to share His message and manage His mysteries. He will give the growth.

A person should consider us in this way: as servants of Christ and managers of God's mysteries. 1 Corinthians 4:1

 Notes and Reflections:

Week 49

- ☐ Monday - 1 Corinthians 15-16
- ☐ Tuesday - 2 Corinthians 1-4
- ☐ Wednesday - 2 Corinthians 5-9
- ☐ Thursday - 2 Corinthians 10-13
- ☐ Friday - Acts 20:1-3; Romans 1-3
- ☐ Saturday - Romans 4-7
- ☐ Sunday - Romans 8-10

Week 50

- ☐ Monday - Romans 11-13
- ☐ Tuesday - Romans 14-16
- ☐ Wednesday - Acts 20:4-38; Acts 21; Acts 22; Acts 23:1-35
- ☐ Thursday - Acts 24-26
- ☐ Friday - Acts 27-28
- ☐ Saturday - Colossians 1-4; Philemon
- ☐ Sunday - Ephesians 1-6

Revelations		
Questions		
Repeats		
Deeper Study		
Etc.		

Suffering Well

As I reflect on my early thirties, I'm met with quite a blur of deep emotion. In the course of a year, I had a friend die from cancer, my Dad had prostate cancer, my daughter had a scary medical ordeal and one of her friends, at the age of four, was diagnosed with a terminal tumor in her brain stem. It was a heavy and difficult time. I've heard God counts each tear that falls, and know He was busy with me during that season. My friends and I would sit, pray and chat about all we were enduring and wonder what in the world God was doing. He never left our sides and gave us strength and courage in situations we never imagined overcoming.

He comforts us in all our affliction, so that we may be able to comfort those who are in any kind of affliction, through the comfort we ourselves receive from God. For as the sufferings of Christ overflow to us, so through Christ our comfort also overflows. 2 Corinthians 1:4-5

Paul expresses this well in Philippians 1:12 when he says, **"Now I want you to know, brothers, that what has happened to me has actually resulted in the advance of the gospel."** Paul was beaten by the crowds, yet God still allowed him to share his testimony with his persecutors (Acts 21-26). He was moved from noble leaders to kings and then from prison to dangerous sea transfers, all while having the opportunity to bend the ear of many audiences including: King Agrippa, Festus, Caesar, Ananias, Felix and even jailers, prison mates and sailors. Paul saw his trials as blessings and took advantage of these audiences to share his great testimony and advance the gospel.

Fast forward over 10 years and I can see that the affliction my friends and I endured offered God the opportunity to provide comfort, strength and courage for us in miraculous ways. Throughout my ministry and life,

I can understand and sympathize with others in ways I would have never been able to without enduring my own trials. As Christ poured out his comfort onto me, I am now able to pour it onto those who cross my path and need compassion and comfort.

We are pressured in every way but not crushed; we are perplexed but not in despair; we are persecuted but not abandoned; we are struck down but not destroyed. 2 Corinthians 4:8-9

A lot was lost during that year and much gained. I was pressed in on every side and clung to God for preservation. I felt slapped to the ground time after time with devastating news, and just when I began to regain my strength, I was knocked down again. But God never forgot me. With His strength and courage I will never let the suffering I endured or the sadness that can still overcome me go to waste. I will use it for His glory and for those He places in my path that need comfort, support and courage. We all still suffer in this world, but surely Paul sets a great example for us all, because he never faltered in his desire to share the good news and love of Christ in the midst of all he endured.

The 3rd Heaven

Boasting is necessary. It is not profitable, but I will move on to visions and revelations of the LORD. I know a man in Christ who was caught up into the third heaven 14 years ago. Whether he was in the body or out of the body, I don't know, God knows. I know that this man— whether in the body or out of the body I don't know, God knows— was caught up into paradise. He heard inexpressible words, which a man is not allowed to speak. 2 Corinthians 12:1-4 What? The third heaven? Right here in the middle of Paul's commentary on

184

boasting, he throws in something unusual I had never noticed. The third heaven? I knew this needed more researching. Eager to understand, I whispered in the middle of our home school classes to a close friend and asked, "What's the deal with this third heaven?" (because sometimes you just can't wait, right?). She didn't have the answer, but we had a quiet discussion about it and both independently researched it later. This is another beautiful thing about the word of God. It sparks conversation, wonder and discussions with others that can bring us closer to Christ.

I discovered that the Jews call the sky first heaven, space and the stars are the second Heaven and everything beyond is referred to as the third heaven. Essentially, the third heaven is what most of us consider heaven and where our Creator and his angels reside.

I had never considered this aspect of Jewish culture. If I've learned nothing else this year, I've discovered that one or two small words can bring great understanding if we pause, reflect and dig deeper into their meaning.

It's quite an example, really. Here Paul is telling the crowds about a man who was caught up in Heaven. He isn't sure if he actually went physically or if it was just a vision, but he is positive he saw paradise and returned to tell about it. Was it what we call a near death experience? Was this man a privileged prophet who was allowed a vision of Heaven? It isn't clear, but I'm thankful those two little words (third heaven) stopped me in my tracks as I read 2 Corinthians and spurred me on to greater knowledge of the Jewish people and the word of God. This is a wonderful example of why the Bible is a living book. Each time I pick it up there is something new to discover or something I've overlooked in the past. I wonder what else God has in store for us this week in our study of His word?

Just One

For just as through one man's disobedience the many were made sinners, so also through the one man's obedience the many will be made righteous. Romans 5:19

What a powerful verse. Through Adam and Eve's disobedience we were all made sinners, but it was through just one man, Jesus, whom we were made righteous once again. To consider the magnitude of this overwhelms me. One man created by God brought sin into the world, and one man, the Son of God, covered all our sin. This truth brings me to my knees in awe before our Lord and Savior.

Now in this hope we were saved, yet hope that is seen is not hope, because who hopes for what he sees? But if we hope for what we do not see, we eagerly wait for it with patience. Romans 8:24-25

We may not see Him, but we do see what He has done and continues to do for each of us when we seek Him. Consider the scripture above. Although we don't see God with our eyes, we can have faith in knowing our salvation is secure because of this one man (Jesus). Understanding this provides more hope than anything else available to us.

On the contrary, what does it say? The message is near you, in your mouth and in your heart. This is the message of faith that we proclaim: If you confess with your mouth, "Jesus is LORD," and believe in your heart that God raised Him from the dead, you will be saved. Romans 10:8-9

Jesus, this one man, is the key to it all. Our salvation and eternal life are wrapped up in the faith and hope we have in Him. God created Adam from dust by speaking him into existence. Adam, in turn, acted with disobedience that made all mankind sinners, but in His love and grace, God sent one man to die so our hope could hold in Him. Just one! Just one man, just one word, just one action, just one thought ... can lead to destruction or to creation. This encourages me to consider what words, actions and thoughts I will choose this week.

A Grand List

Love must be without hypocrisy. Detest evil; cling to what is good. Show family affection to one another with brotherly love. Outdo one another in showing honor. Do not lack diligence; be fervent in spirit; serve the LORD. Rejoice in hope; be patient in affliction; be persistent in prayer. Share with the saints in their needs; pursue hospitality. Bless those who persecute you; bless and do not curse. Rejoice with those who rejoice; weep with those who weep. Be in agreement with one another. Do not be proud; instead, associate with the humble. Do not be wise in your own estimation. Do not repay anyone evil for evil. Try to do what is honorable in everyone's eyes. [18] If possible, on your part, live at peace with everyone. Friends, do not avenge yourselves; instead, leave room for His wrath. For it is written: Vengeance belongs to Me; I will repay, says the LORD. But, If your enemy is hungry, feed him. If he is thirsty, give him something to drink. For in so doing you will be heaping fiery coals on his head. Do not be conquered by evil, but conquer evil with good. Romans 12:9-21

These powerful verses speak for themselves. This is a grand list concerning Christian ethics and a very tall order for human flesh. I read it several times, trying to allow it to sink into my heart. It stirred up great emotion within me, as much of God's word does. Mostly, it brings me to my knees and my heart to pray as I consider how I fall so short in mastering God's instructions. Thankfully, because of His great word, we can know and trust He will stick with us, guide us, rebuke us and love us on the path that leads to Him.

Older Women

With a daughter in middle school, I'm often meeting new friends and their families. I often ask myself what my actions and words reflect about God when I'm around the curious ears of these young ladies. Honestly, some days my answer is better than others. As I arrived in Titus 2 this week, I was reminded of Paul's instructive words in one of the pastoral epistles.

In the same way, older women are to be reverent in behavior, not slanderers, not addicted to much wine. They are to teach what is good, so they may encourage the young women to love their husbands and to love their children, to be self-controlled, pure, homemakers, kind, and submissive to their husbands, so that God's message will not be slandered. Titus 2:3-5

There are many who will take offense, as I once did, to the words homemaker and submission, but let's not allow the world's negative connotations to these words keep our eyes and hearts from receiving wisdom from the Lord.

I'd also like to point out that Paul's use of the words "older women" is not necessarily referring to women in their 80s. While God has placed older women in my life to teach me His ways, likewise, I am also considered an "older woman" to those He has placed in my life who are younger than I. Being "older" is different from being "old." Anytime we can help model for young women how to be a Godly woman, wife, sister, friend and mom — we should, since it's exactly what Christ is calling us to here in Titus 2. .

Since you know my affinity for lists, you're probably not surprised that I appreciate Paul's clear advice on how to be an encouragement and example of Christ to those we come in contact with. Basically, he offers a relational guidebook for Christian women. Let's break it down:

- Be reverent. Simply put, be devoted and respectful of others.
- Don't gossip or talk negatively about others.
- Don't drink too much, teach only good things and encourage women to love their husbands and children, rather than speak negatively about them.
- Practice self-control, purity and kindness. Manage your household and care for your family, while yielding to your husband.

How do you feel as you read this list? I'm feeling convicted to my core in several areas, and plan to make every effort to pray for myself in these areas of weakness so that I can be the role model God intends for me to be. I want to leave a legacy that includes all of these qualities and inspires others to come alongside and do the same. Will you join me?

Week 51

- ☐ Monday - Philippians 1-4
- ☐ Tuesday - 1 Timothy 1-6
- ☐ Wednesday - Titus 1-3
- ☐ Thursday - 1 Peter 1-5
- ☐ Friday - Hebrews 1-6
- ☐ Saturday - Hebrews 7-10
- ☐ Sunday - Hebrews 11-13

Week 52

- ☐ Monday - 2 Timothy 1-4
- ☐ Tuesday - 2 Peter 1-3; Jude
- ☐ Wednesday - 1 John 1-5
- ☐ Thursday - 2 John; 3 John
- ☐ Friday - Revelation 1-5
- ☐ Saturday - Revelation 6-15
- ☐ Sunday – Revelation 16-22

Revelations	
Questions	
Repeats	
Deeper Study	
Etc.	

A Living Stone

We often hear the message that Christ is our cornerstone and foundation. However, as I read 1 Peter, I noticed these verses that express how we should look at ourselves as living stones.

... You have tasted that the LORD is good. Coming to Him, a living stone—rejected by men but chosen and valuable to God—you yourselves, as living stones, are being built into a spiritual house for a holy priesthood to offer spiritual sacrifices acceptable to God through Jesus Christ. 1 Peter 2:3-5

We always hear the call to be the hands and feet of Christ or the body of Christ, but have you ever considered being a "living stone" of His spiritual house? I adore this imagery. Imagining each one of God's children working together and building upon one another, making the house stronger with each person we add to the family.

When we camp in the mountains, we search for stones to build Cairns. These carefully arranged piles of rocks guide hikers in areas where there are no trees or where visibility is poor. We just make them for fun, but have to search carefully for each stone to make sure it fits perfectly in size and shape in preparation for the next level. No stone could be the same in creating this tower. If we didn't use varying shapes and sizes of rocks, the construction would have failed. Similarly, God has uniquely created us to complete a distinct mission and fulfill His divine purpose. When we do this, we guide others who are lost towards Christ and begin to open their eyes to His glory and love so they can experience life as a "living stone."

Incredible! What does it look like to work together as "living stones" and build upon each others' strengths and grow God's spiritual house?

I imagine God's purpose is fulfilled when we come together in love, not in competition or judgement, and use the spiritual gifts and talents that

192

God has given each of us to share the Gospel. Not being jealous of someone else's gifts and talents, but coming alongside them with the gifts God has blessed us with. Not comparing our abilities to others, but doing what we can and accepting what God has given us and left out of our lives. Not grumbling about the sacrifices we have to make, but giving thanks for the opportunity we have to be a part of God's spiritual house.

God never said this would be easy. Being a living stone of His spiritual house will take more strength, courage, wisdom and humility than we could ever imagine. The beauty of God's plan and love is that He never created us to do anything alone. All we have to do is call on Him, trust in Him and lean on Him for all we need to carry out His will and grow His house. I'm in! How about you?

Mighty Reminders

As life flies by, it can be difficult to sit and revel in the rich inheritance that we have gained through Christ. I found these short, but rich nuggets of truth this week as my journey through the Bible comes to a close (this time around). I'm keeping it short in the hope that you will sit and savor these three reminders of all that we gained through Christ's death. For we have truly been rescued and redeemed by an almighty God who loves us more than we can fathom. He has erased all our sin and given us more than we could ever dream.

May you be strengthened with all power, according to His glorious might, for all endurance and patience, with joy giving thanks to the Father, who has enabled you to share in the saints' inheritance in the light. He has rescued us from the domain of darkness and transferred us into the kingdom of the Son He loves. Colossians 1:11-13

He erased the certificate of debt, with its obligations, that was against us and opposed to us, and has taken it out of the way by nailing it to the cross. Colossians 2:14

For you know that you were redeemed from your empty way of life inherited from the fathers, not with perishable things like silver or gold, but with the precious blood of Christ, like that of a lamb without defect or blemish. 1 Peter 1:18-19

Our Anchor

We have this hope as an anchor for our lives, safe and secure. It enters the inner sanctuary behind the curtain. Jesus has entered there on our behalf as a forerunner, because He has become a high priest forever in the order of Melchizedek. Hebrews 6:19-20

Mel who? I'm not sure how many times I've skipped over Melchizedek while reading the Bible before, but this time it really piqued my interest. Other than in Hebrews, the mysterious order of Melchizedek is only mentioned two other times: once in Genesis and not again until Psalm 110. So I had to dig a little deeper. Who is this high priest? After all, Jesus is a high priest in the order of Melchizedek, so he must be important.

After Abram returned from defeating Chedorlaomer and the kings who were with him, the king of Sodom went out to meet him in the Valley of Shaveh (that is, the King's Valley). Then Melchizedek, king of Salem, brought out bread and wine; he was a priest to God Most High. Genesis 14:17-18

194

The LORD has sworn an oath and will not take it back: "Forever, You are a priest like Melchizedek." Psalm 110:4

Here is what we know from scripture. He was a priest who served God Himself. It says there is no record of his birth or death, leading some to believe he is divine, and his name means king of Salem and king of Peace.

For this Melchizedek—

King of Salem, priest of the Most High God,
who met Abraham and blessed him
as he returned from defeating the kings,
and Abraham gave him a tenth of everything;
first, his name means king of righteousness,
then also, king of Salem,
meaning king of peace;

without father, mother, or genealogy,
having neither beginning of days nor end of life,
but resembling the Son of God— remains a priest forever.
Hebrews 7:1-3

As with most mysteries, there are several schools of thought on who Melchizedek really was.

Some think he was Jesus, some the archangel Michael, others think he was just an ordinary human. The Hebrew tradition tells us it was Shem, Noah's Son that was still alive at the time of Abraham. This would certainly make him be the oldest man alive qualifying him as a candidate for the order of Melchizedek.

Apparently, there is even a Dead Sea scroll that says Melchizedek will be the one to carry out God's judgements and delivers His people from the hands of Satan.

I went down the rabbit hole and spent over an hour reading different commentaries and thoughts on Melchizedek. This is one of those things we won't know for certain until we reach Heaven, but it's also a great example of what keeps me coming back to God's word. There is always a surprise, mystery and truth to discover. I encourage you to do some searching on your own about the greatness of Melchizedek.

By Faith

We don't know for certain who the author of Hebrews is, but I couldn't help but read in awe of the grand list and recap (in Hebrews 11) of all faith has done and accomplished for the Kingdom of God. Not only that, all of these people were just like you and me. They were made of flesh, subject to temptation and fell to sin; but with faith they overcame and were living examples of what faith can accomplish, what it looks like and how God honors his those who love him. We have read most of these stories in the Bible, but what a powerful testimony of God's grace to see this sampling of faithful servants listed out!

But what about our own lives? Have you considered your own life and the ways you have acted "by faith?"

I'm going to take some time this week to think about all the things in my own life where I acted "by faith" and write out the ways God responded. Maybe you will consider doing it yourself? I can't imagine all the things I've forgotten or overlooked. Praying He will remind us all of the fruit of our faith and that we can continue to add to this list all the days of our lives.

Read, reflect and count all of the "By Faith" statements you encounter in Hebrews 11.

Spin Cycle

But know this: Difficult times will come in the last days. For people will be lovers of self, lovers of money, boastful, proud, blasphemers, disobedient to parents, ungrateful, unholy, unloving, irreconcilable, slanderers, without self-control, brutal, without love for what is good, traitors, reckless, conceited, lovers of pleasure rather than lovers of God, holding to the form of godliness but denying its power. Avoid these people! 2 Timothy 3:1-5

Avoid these people? "How?" I wrote in the margin of my Bible. How can I avoid all these people when they seem to surround me? Now, I'm not trying to say I'm never any of these things, because I'm just as flesh and blood as everyone else. However, the media, commercials, songs, business owners and politicians seem to fill the news and airwaves with every one of these items on a constant spin cycle. It's overwhelming. In fact, I reached the point a few weeks ago where I was so totally drained by the world, I felt spiritually empty. I had poured it out and poured it out, but forgotten to surround myself with other believers to fill up. Church, Bible study and small group are not enough! I prayed and hibernated for a few days, when God answered my prayers in a mighty way by giving me an emergency refill of deep and meaningful "Jesus" talk. He brought true Christian friends into my path on Friday, Sunday, and twice on Monday. It renewed me and helped me realize how I had neglected to recharge with those who are like-minded. We are called to serve and be the light to those who surround us at work, in our neighborhoods, community and even churches. However, we are only able to serve if we are filled up because we will face evil and the deceiver will try to shut us down with exhaustion, frustration or guilt. We need reserves for that so we don't fall victim to the persecution and deception.

In fact, all those who want to live a godly life in Christ Jesus will be persecuted. Evil people and impostors will become worse, deceiving and being deceived. 2 Timothy 3:12-13

We must remember to fill up, not just at church and small group, but through time with God and close friends, family and co-workers whom we can sit down with and share meaningful Biblical discussions. This is vital to our hearts and minds so that we have the knowledge, strength and courage to proclaim God's love with grace and patience.

Proclaim the message; persist in it whether convenient or not; rebuke, correct, and encourage with great patience and teaching. 2 Timothy 4:2

Conscience Condemnation

Last summer we were at an event where a friend asked me a question concerning a conversation we had started earlier in the day. Unfortunately, another friend, who hadn't heard our previous conversation, didn't understand the context of my comment and was offended. She graciously left the conversation never saying a word. However, a few days later, another friend told me how it had upset her and I felt horrible. Honestly, I didn't sleep very well for a few nights and finally just called her to see if I could come over to talk. I shared the "entire" story and apologized for hurting her feelings. She received it with the gracious nature I always see her display. She explained that she was fine and was sorry that I had been so upset by it.

Dear friends, if our conscience doesn't condemn us, we have confidence before God and can receive whatever we ask from Him because we keep His commands and do what is pleasing in His sight. Now this is His command: that we believe in the name of His Son Jesus Christ, and love one another as He commanded us. 1 John 3:21-23

The definition of conscience is the part of the mind that makes you aware of your actions as being either morally right or wrong; a feeling that something you have done is morally wrong.

I'm certainly not saying we shouldn't do the right thing, right a wrong that has been done or apologize. When the Holy Spirit tugs on our hearts, we should respond to seek forgiveness and restoration in relationships. What I want to highlight is that our conscience will often trick us into thinking we aren't good enough for God's love, forgiveness and grace. It takes over as judge and jury while we sit on trial, but that is God's place. We are almost always harder on ourselves than anyone else could ever be. That's why it was like a flashlight was spotlighting verse 21 for me.

"If our conscience doesn't condemn us, we have confidence before God and can …"

We may let go of God because our shame and guilt build up a wall around our hearts. We may let go of God because we feel like our past is too broken or we aren't good enough. We may let go of God, but He

199

never lets go of us. Let's not let our conscience condemn us! Condemnation is not from the Lord, but stems from Satan and his lies. Let's trust in God's word and trust in the One who breathed life into man and placed the stars in the sky. Let's trust in His love for us and give thanks for His past and present provision, so we can stand with confidence at His throne in the final days.

Letters to the Angels

In the book of Revelation (chapters 2-3) we discover letters which are written to the angels of the seven churches. I find this fascinating. Letters to angels! Scholars believe these seven churches were chosen because they were the first churches to provide the Gospel to all the other churches that followed. Each of the seven letters seems to follow a similar format consisting of: an introduction, a compliment, a condemnation and a command to correct the problem addressed. It's so fascinating! Today we will focus on the complaint of the church of Laodicea.

"Write to the angel of the church in Laodicea:

"The Amen, the faithful and true Witness, the Originator of God's creation says: I know your works, that you are neither cold nor hot. I wish that you were cold or hot. So, because you are lukewarm, and neither hot nor cold, I am going to vomit you out of My mouth. Revelation 3:14-16

The complaint against this church was that their people were essentially somewhere in the middle of Christianity. They believed, but were not passionate and all in. This letter clearly instructs that mediocre living isn't enough! Lukewarm is defined as slightly warm or warmish. Do we want to be known as "slightly" Christian or "Christianish"? I certainly do not. In fact, I hear from women all the time that the reason they aren't going to church is because they had some friends who were "Christians" and they weren't very kind or lived wild lives. I've heard from single women who have chosen to date men who don't attend church because the ones they have dated that do attend church aren't very nice. This is when I say that "Christianish" people make sharing the Gospel with others more difficult than most atheists do.

I was greatly convicted by this reminder that God would rather us either be hot or cold, instead of somewhere in the middle. When we are in the word of God, the call is clear and our convictions can be strong. I deeply desire to have the Father sitting at my table. How about you?

Reflect on Revelation 3:17-22.

Are we the Prostitute?

As I studied Revelation 17 and 18 this week, I could not help but think of the United States when I read **about "Babylon the Great, the Mother of Prostitutes and of the vile things of the Earth." (Rev. 17:5)** The similarities are more than a bit disconcerting.

He also said to me, "The waters you saw, where the prostitute was seated, are peoples, multitudes, nations, and languages (Rev. 17:15). This nation prides itself in being a melting pot.

For all the nations have drunk the wine of her sexual immorality, which brings wrath. The kings of the earth have committed sexual

immorality with her, and the merchants of the earth have grown wealthy from her excessive luxury (Rev. 18:3). This nation has been the world leader in all things for centuries. The nation who comes to the aid of all and buys from all over, creating wealth for other nations as we live in excess, having more than we would ever need.

As much as she glorified herself and lived luxuriously, give her that much torment and grief, for she says in her heart, "I sit as a queen; I am not a widow, and I will never see grief" (v. 7). We have lived luxuriously and are accused of having a great arrogance about our power, safety, influence and importance.

I urge you to read these chapters and see what you think. I'm no theologian, but that shouldn't keep any of us from picking up God's word and asking questions, researching and discussing. Because, no matter what other great theologians may say, only God truly knows the message behind the mysterious book of Revelation. So, maybe I'm way off here, but this prostitute sounds uncannily similar to our countr,y and I've found it greatly disturbing. As we continue through Revelation 18, we see the great destruction that comes to this prostitute as God judges her with His mighty wrath for all her evil ways.

Read Revelation 18:11-21.

I'm no end times scholar, but I have lived in the United States all my life. I know the history and faith in which the country was founded, and I know the ways and laws of our Heavenly Father and Creator. I can see how my country has fallen away from the ways and laws of God, and it's unnerving. I see that hate, jealousy, rage, deception, sexual immorality, false teachings and selfish pride that seem to be seeping into every pore of this nation. Are we the prostitute? If we are not, we certainly could

202

be. The hope I have is that, just like the prostitute by the well that Jesus gave forgiveness and His Living Water, we as a nation may still have the chance to acknowledge Christ and turn back to Him for that same grace.

Final Thoughts and Revelations

I can't believe we have completed the year of reading the Bible chronologically. There were days the story was fascinating and thrilling, and others when I wondered if I would ever make it through (Leviticus and Job). If you had told me I would say that about studying God's word several years ago, I wouldn't have believed you, but it's true. It's difficult to explain how amazing this journey has been for me. Even on the weeks containing more than four or five devotions, I still left out so much I highlighted, studied and starred in my Bible. However, if I had to boil it all down to three main themes to tuck away in my heart to ponder daily, it would be these:

This is how we are sure that we have come to know Him: by keeping His commands. The one who says, "I have come to know Him," yet doesn't keep His commands, is a liar, and the truth is not in him. But whoever keeps His word, truly in him the love of God is perfected. This is how we know we are in Him.

1 John 2:3-5

1. Know and obey God's commands. To know them, we must read His word so that we know the commands. To keep and obey them, we have to read His word so we know to lean, ask and

trust in our Heavenly Father for the strength, discipline and faith to follow Him.

So now, little children, remain in Him, so that when He appears we may have boldness and not be ashamed before Him at His coming. 1 John 2:28

2. It's not about this world, but our eternal one. We get so caught up in the "wants" that we forget to focus on all our needs God is meeting daily. If we will remain in God through His word, we have a greater chance of overcoming idols and taking the narrow gate that will lead us to Him, so that we can enjoy eternal life with our Savior who died to cover all our sins, faults and failures.

Anyone who does not remain in Christ's teaching but goes beyond it, does not have God. The one who remains in that teaching, this one has both the Father and the Son. 2 John 1:9

3. If we are to have eternal life with our Heavenly Father, we must believe in His Son Jesus, and when we know the Father, we must remain in His teaching. If we know the Father and turn away from Him, we are no better than those who never believed.

I pray this year of reading the Bible has encouraged and convicted you in astounding ways as it did me. I will never be the same, and I'm so grateful I was given the incentive to read with a friend over the year. So, today, I want to encourage you to share your experiences of reading the Bible chronologically with someone you know. Maybe buy them a chronological Bible or print out a chronological reading plan to encourage and get them started? In fact, I loved it so much, I'm preparing to do it all over again this year. After all, who doesn't desire to know more about our **"God who holds your life-breath in His hands and who controls the whole course of your life?" (Daniel 5:23)**

Praying we all continue to seek our Heavenly Father through His written word. It never fails and is always relevant.
It lives and breathes after all these centuries and will continue to do so until His return and all that was prophesied is accomplished.

Made in the USA
Columbia, SC
28 July 2019